A GUIDE TO
WRITERS' HOMES
IN NEW ENGLAND

A GUIDE TO WRITERS' HOMES IN NEW ENGLAND

MIRIAM LEVINE

Illustrations by Tom Siebert

1984
Apple-wood Books
Cambridge • *Watertown*

All possible care has been taken to make full acknowledgment in every case where material is still in copyright. If errors have occurred, they will be corrected with full apology in subsequent editions if notification is sent to the publisher.

Grateful acknowledgment is made for permission to reprint the following: *The Centenary Edition of the Works of Nathaniel Hawthorne*, Vol. VIII, "The American Notebooks." Copyright © 1972 by Ohio State University Press. Reprinted by permission of Ohio State University Press. *The Letters of Emily Dickinson*, edited by Thomas H. Johnson. Copyright © 1958 by the President and Fellows of Harvard College. Reprinted by permission of The Belknap Press of Harvard University Press. *The Letters of Herman Melville*, edited by Merrell R. Davis and William H. Gilman. Copyright © 1960 by Yale University Press. *Louisa May: A Modern Biography of Louisa May Alcott* by Martha Saxton. Copyright © 1977 by Martha Saxton. Reprinted by permission of Houghton Mifflin Company. *Mark Twain's Letters*, edited by Albert Bigelow Paine. Copyright © 1917, © 1945 by Harper and Row. Reprinted by permission of Harper and Row. *Selected Letters of Robert Frost*, edited by Lawrence Thompson. Copyright © by Lawrence Thompson. Reprinted by permission of Holt, Rinehart and Winston. Journal of Amos Bronson Alcott. Reprinted by permission of Houghton Library, Harvard University. Diary of Louisa May Alcott. Reprinted by permission of Houghton Library, Harvard University. Letter of Helen Hunt Jackson. Reprinted by permission of Houghton Library, Harvard University. Letters of Fanny Appleton Longfellow. Reprinted by permission of the Department of the Interior, Longfellow National Historic Site. Diary of Sarah Orne Jewett. Reprinted by permission of Houghton Library, Harvard University. Letter of Calvin Stowe. Reprinted by permission of The Stowe-Day Foundation.

ISBN 0-918222-51-6

2 3 4 5 6 7 8 9 0

To The Reader

We have made every effort to insure that the information included in this guide is correct and up-to-date. The information included in this edition is current as of the spring of 1984. Please note, however, that prices and hours of opening at the homes are subject to change. When using this book, we recommend that you call ahead, in order to avoid disappointment or dissatisfaction. Please note that the description of each of the writers' homes featured in this book begins with practical information such as hours of opening, admission charges, exhibits or details of note, and is followed by a chronology of the writer's life. Within the chronology, rather than repeating the writer's name, we have used his or her initials. In order to further help place the writer in the home, we have printed the years in which the writer lived at the house in boldface type. We hope this book provides great pleasure.

Apple-wood Books

Acknowledgments

Thanks to the following people who have helped with this book in various ways: John Lane; Phil Zuckerman; Stephen Love; Sarita Jacobson; Betty Howard; Frank Buda, Head Guide, Longfellow National Historic Site; Gerard Chapman; John Butterfield, Guide, Orchard House; Kathy Catalando, Curator, Longfellow National Historic Site; Margaret Cheney, Curator, The Mark Twain House; Julia Cole, Guide, Orchard House; Robert Derry, Site Supervisor, The Wayside; Donna Donnelly, Guide, The Mark Twain House; Jayne Gordon, Director, Orchard House; Bruce Harrison, Caretaker, The William Cullen Bryant Homestead; Michelle Hodgdon, Resident Overseer, The Sarah Orne Jewett House; Julie Irving, The Wadsworth-Longfellow House; Anthony King, Director, Arrowhead; Margaret Laible, Administrator, The Old Manse; Gregory Laing, Special Collections, Haverhill Public Library; Lois Erickson McDonald, Associate Curator, Monte Cristo Cottage; Janice McGroary, Assistant Director, Frost Place; Mary Misch, Executive Secretary, The Mount; Debra Marts Moore, Caretaker, The John Greenleaf Whittier Home; S. Kenneth Paulsen, Guide, Monte Cristo Cottage; Sally Thomas Pavetti, Curator, Monte Cristo Cottage; Jo-Anne Randall, Manager, The Robert Frost Farm; Richard S. Reed, Director, Fruitlands Museum; Mary Kate Sampson, Guide, Longfellow National Historic Site; Freda Sass, Guide, Arrowhead; Ellice Schofield, Curator, The Stowe-Day Foundation; Bette B. Sheatsley, Director, The Ralph Waldo Emerson House.

Contents

Preface

When I began collecting material for this guide to writers' homes in New England, I concentrated on practical traveler's information: addresses, phone numbers, hours, admission charges, parking information, and special points of interest. However, the more I learned about the lives of the writers, the more interesting my visits to their houses became. To give the traveler and reader a complete picture of what life must have been like in these houses, I've included biographical essays describing each writer's private and public life during the years of his or her residence. I found that the architecture, decor, and gardens, which I also describe, almost always reflect the personalities of the writers and their families. In their letters, journals, and diaries, I discovered everyday concerns similar to ours. Their subjects were our subjects: money, sex, work, family, friends, shelter, and food.

Writers work at home, moving back and forth between the privacy of their studies and their domestic lives. I was fascinated to discover how they supported and were supported by their families. For instance, Melville's sisters worked as his copyists; Emily Dickinson's sister managed the household; Thoreau's mother did his laundry; Louisa May Alcott, Sarah Orne Jewett, Harriet Beecher Stowe, and Edith Wharton were all the principal wage earners in their families. In this book, I've tried to show how these great writers' work lives and domestic lives were entangled, and how they were shaped by the houses which contained them.

Miriam Levine
Arlington, Massachusetts
April, 1984

Connecticut

The Mark Twain House
Hartford, Connecticut

Samuel Clemens

Samuel Clemens

351 Farmington Avenue
Hartford, Connecticut 06105
203-247-0998

Open year round. June 1-August 31, 10 am-4:30 pm, Daily; September 1-
May 31, 9:30 am-4 pm, Tuesday through Saturday, 1 pm-4 pm, Sunday;
Closed January 1, Easter, Labor Day, Thanksgiving, December 24 and 25.
Tours daily. Separate and combination admission with the Harriet
Beecher Stowe House is available. Admission — Twain house: Adults,
$3.50; Children 16 and under, $1.50; Preschoolers, no charge. Twain and
Stowe House: Adults, $5.75; Children 16 and under, $2.75; Preschoolers,
no charge. Parking in the lot next to the Mark Twain House on Farming-
ton Avenue. A stairway leads from the parking lot to the grounds of the
Visitors' Center, The Mark Twain House, and The Harriet Beecher Stowe
House. Tours for both houses begin at the Visitors' Center (77 Forest
Street). The display at the Visitors' Center offers a helpful illustrated his-
tory of the Nook Farm community.

1835. Born in Florida, Missouri, November 30, to Jane Lampton Clemens
and John Marshall Clemens.
1857. SC becomes an apprentice pilot on the Mississippi River.
1864. SC joins the San Francisco *Morning Call.*
1867. *The Celebrated Jumping Frog of Calaveras County* is published.
1870. SC marries Oliva Langdon of Elmira, New York, on February 2. They
live in Buffalo. SC works as an editor of the *Express.* First child, Langdon Clemens born.
1872. Suzy Clemens born. *Roughing It* published. June 2, Langdon Clemens dies.
**1874. Clemenses move into new house on Farmington
Avenue in Hartford. Clara Clemens born.**
1876. *The Adventures of Tom Sawyer* published.
1880. Third daughter, Jean, born. *A Tramp Abroad* published.
**1881. Kitchen wing is added to SC's Hartford house. First
floor is redecorated by Associated Artists. *The Prince and
the Pauper* published.**
**1891. The Clemenses move to Europe after severe financial
losses.**
1896. Around-the-world lecture tour. Suzy Clemens dies in Hartford,
August 18.
1903. Hartford home is sold.
1910. Dies, April 21 in Redding, Connecticut.

Samuel Clemens had grown up poor and always longed for the protective and magical power of great wealth. With his marriage to Olivia Langdon, he entered the upper-middle class. On his wedding night in 1870, Clemens believed that he and Olivia were on their way to an ordinary rooming house; instead, the coachman took them to a fashionable address in Buffalo. Olivia led him up the steps of a splendid brick townhouse where his father-in-law, flushed with the pleasure of generosity, handed him the deed to the completely furnished, equipped, and staffed mansion. Coachman, cook, and housemaid lined up like servant-helpers in a fairy tale, waiting to serve the commoner who had married the king's daughter.

However, within two years, Clemens began dreaming of building an even more opulent house in Hartford, Connecticut. He was attracted to the solid, respectable town which, at that time, had the highest per-capita income of any city in America. Thomas Beecher, the brother of Harriet Beecher Stowe, introduced him to their sister, Isabella Beecher Hooker, a prominent hostess. She and her husband, John Hooker, lived on the western edge of town in the stylish Nook Farm area; John Hooker had bought one hundred acres and then sold off parcels to people he approved of. The Beechers had reservations about Samuel Clemens, the newly-arrived social climber, but because of Olivia's connections and money, the Clemenses were allowed to buy land.

In 1872, Olivia and Samuel Clemens hired Edward Tuckerman Potter to design their new house, which would cost them $122,000. The surprising exterior of the High-Victorian-Gothic house reflects Clemens's exuberant personality and originality: broken elevations; five balconies; three turrets; a shaded porch, called the "Ombra," which curves around the house; brick walls inlaid with designs in scarlet and black; and the roof, also patterned in colored designs. The interior plan is more conventional. On the first floor an entrance hall leads to four large rooms in a rectangle: front drawing room and dining room on the right, library and front guestroom on the left. In all, there are nineteen rooms and five baths.

In 1874, Clemens moved into his castle: a magical, comforting retreat, which gave him the illusion that nothing bad would ever happen. It was his idea to divert the chimney over the dining room fireplace so that a window could be installed and he could see the snow falling over a blazing red fire. He had tin roofing installed on certain sections of the house so that he could hear the sound of falling rain. With these theatrical effects and a conservatory filled with lilies blooming in winter around a gently splashing fountain, Clemens created an atmosphere of fire, light, snow, rain, flowers: nature tamed and safely beautiful, an enchanted kingdom dreamed by a poor boy.

His need for control extended to his children. He was deeply, and sometimes unhealthily, connected to his three daughters, Suzy, Clara, and Jean, but especially to Suzy, who was born after the death of the Clemenses' first child, Langdon. Afraid of losing another child, he and Olivia anxiously over-protected her.

Olivia tutored her daughters in the large schoolroom on the second floor, over the library. Each child did lessons at her own desk and, on dark winter days, read or drew by the light of her own desk lamp. There was a children's bathroom with child-sized fixtures—including a small zinc tub—right off Clara and Jean's bedroom, which connected to the schoolroom. After school, the children invited their mob of dolls for an afternoon tea party.

Only their father's rages disturbed the children's small enclosed world. All their lives they had been afraid of his violent and unpredictable temper. He was only happy with his children when they were his subjects and he played the generous king. On Suzy's third birthday, according to Clemens, he and Olivia and the servants "got up a rousing wood fire in the main hall...illuminated the place with a rich glow from all the globes of the newell chandelier, spread a bright rug before the fire, set a circling row of chairs (pink ones and dove-colored)." Then they heaped the low table with presents: "a pink azalea in lavish bloom...a Russia-leather bible...a gold ring...a silver thimble...a rattling mob of Sunday clad dolls..." and his personal gift, a Noah's Ark with 200 wooden animals.

He and Olivia loved to spend. In 1879, they came back from

Europe with crates of furniture; the largest held a massive, Venetian, black-walnut bed with cherubs carved on the removable finials of the bedposts. In 1881, they bought an adjoining strip of land; rerouted the driveway; rebuilt the kitchen, doubling its size; enlarged the front hall; and installed new plumbing and heating, as well as a burglar alarm. Clemens also had the grounds relandscaped, in order to create a more dramatic view of the house.

In the same year, they hired the firm of Associated Artists (Louis Tiffany, Samuel Colman, Lockwood de Forest and Candace Wheeler) to redecorate the first floor. They brightened the house by applying stenciled designs, adapted from American Indian, Moorish, and Chinese sources, to the dark, Victorian woodwork and to the walls. The colors were richly muted: silver on the red walls in the entrance hall which looked like a sultan's tent with its center pillar, pale rose-beige on silvery gray in the drawing room, and gold on blue in the library. The effect was subtle and precious.

The Clemenses lived like aristocrats. Even when they dined alone—which was rarely—they dressed formally for dinner. Olivia usually chose gowns of blue or red silk which set off her dark hair and eyes and her exquisitely white skin. After dinner they often rode out in the same carriage that Olivia's father had given them, driven by the same coachman who had taken them to their new home on their wedding night in Buffalo. In the deepening twilight, they would return home, the house lit, the silver and crystal shining, the servants ready to welcome the master and mistress.

Extravagant, indulgent hosts, the Clemenses shared their pleasures. The first-floor guest room, which a friend called the royal chamber, was more richly decorated than the master bedroom and had its own private entrance. The imposing canopied bed, the other furniture, the moldings, the baseboards, and the paneling were all mahogany. The private bath was fitted with two marble-topped sinks and a huge bathtub, all set in mahogany. The dressing room had a fireplace where guests could warm themselves after their winter baths.

Dinner parties were lavish: soup first, then fillet of beef or canvasback duck, sherry, claret, champagne, and creme de menthe with coffee. There were two, sometimes three kinds of dessert: charlotte russe, Nesselrode pudding, and, often, ice cream, always molded in wonderful shapes of flowers and cherubs. Clemens held court during dinner, charming and dominating his guests with story after story.

The dinner parties, the teas, the visiting celebrities, the exquisite interiors distracted Clemens. He couldn't work at Nook Farm. He abandoned the large, bright room over the library which he had originally intended for his study and retreated to a small, plain room over the coachhouse, which turned out to be too small. He then moved his desk back to the main house, to the third-floor billiard room. But even here, secluded at the top of the house, he wrote little.

Only during the summer could he find the absolute quiet he needed. He did almost all of his writing away from Nook Farm, at his sister-in-law's summer house in Elmira, New York. She had built him a private, one-room, octagonal house with windows on all sides, one hundred yards from the main house.

In addition to his writing, Samuel Clemens tried various schemes to make more money. From the 1880s on, believing he would make at least twenty million dollars a year, he began to invest more and more heavily in the Paige typesetter, eventually guaranteeing to finance and promote its manufacture.

In 1884, with *Huckleberry Finn* as the first book, he began his own publishing company. Unwisely, he drew off the profits, leaving this business undercapitalized so he could finance the typesetter, which had become his obsession. Charmed by its inventor and susceptible to the lure of immense wealth, Clemens poured more and more money into perfecting the machine, which kept breaking down, until in 1891, the other backers, disgusted, withdrew, and Clemens, to save money, closed up the fabulous house in Nook Farm and took his family to Europe. In 1894, his publishing company went into bankruptcy.

In 1896, in exile abroad, trying to earn money to pay off his creditors, Clemens received news of his daughter Suzy's death. She had been staying in Hartford with former neighbors when she became ill with spinal meningitis. She lived her last two weeks in the first floor guest room of her old house, cared for by the Clemens' maid, Katy Leary. In delirium, losing her sight, Suzy wrote to her father: "I see that even darkness can be great. To me darkness must remain from everlasting to everlasting." Trying to find some consolation, Clemens wrote from London:

> Suzy died at *home* . . . If she had died in another house — well, I think I could not have borne that. To us, our house was not unsentient matter — it had a heart, and a soul, and eyes to see us with . . . and we could not enter it unmoved.

Still grieving when she returned from abroad in 1900, Olivia could not bear to live in the Farmington Avenue house. In 1903, it was sold to Richard M. Bissell, the President of the Hartford Fire Insurance Company, who lived there with his family until renting the house to The Kingswood School for Boys in 1917. In 1922, the house was sold, used as a coal warehouse, and later subdivided into apartments. The Mark Twain Memorial Committee, chaired by Katharine Seymour Day, bought the house from the City Coal Company in 1929, and is responsible for the subsequent restoration which took almost twenty years, from 1955 to 1974.

The Harriet Beecher Stowe House

Hartford, Connecticut

Harriet Beecher Stowe

Harriet Beecher Stowe

73 Forest Street
Hartford, Connecticut 06105
203-525-9317

Open year round. June 1-August 31, 10 am-4:30 pm, daily; September 1-
May 31, 9:30 am-4 pm, Tuesday through Saturday, 1 pm-4 pm, Sunday;
Closed January 1, Easter, Labor Day, Thanksgiving, December 24 and 25.
Tours daily. Separate and combination admission with the Mark Twain
House is available. Admission — Stowe house: Adults, $2.75; Children 16
and under, $1.25; Preschoolers, no charge. Twain and Stowe House:
Adults, $5.75; Children 16 and under, $2.75; Preschoolers, no charge. Park-
ing in the lot next to the Mark Twain House on Farmington Avenue. A
stairway leads from the parking lot to the grounds of the Visitors' Center,
The Mark Twain House, and The Harriet Beecher Stowe House. Tours for
both houses begin at the Visitors' Center (77 Forest Street). The display at
the Visitors' Center offers a helpful illustrated history of the Nook Farm
community. Exceptional garden with many varieties of plants familiar to
Harriet Beecher Stowe.

1811. Born June 14, in Litchfield, Connecticut, seventh child of Roxana
    Foote Beecher and Lyman Beecher.
1816. HBS's mother dies.
1818. HBS's father marries Harriet Porter.
1824. HBS attends female seminary in Hartford run by her sister,
    Catherine.
1836. HBS marries Calvin Ellis Stowe, Professor of Biblical Literature at
    Lane Theological Seminary in Cincinnati, where HBS's father is
    president.
1843. *The Mayflower, or Sketches of Scenes and Characters Among the
    Descendants of the Pilgrims,* HBS's first book of fiction, is published.
1850. Charles, HBS's seventh and last child, is born in Brunswick, Maine,
    where Calvin Stowe teaches at Bowdoin College.
1853. HBS takes the first of three trips to Europe.
1857. Henry, HBS's first son, drowns.
1859. *The Minister's Wooing,* a novel, HBS's ninth book, is published. She
    continues to be the main support of her family.
1864. HBS moves to Hartford, builds Oakholm, an Italianate-Tudor villa.
1868. HBS buys winter home in Mandarin, Florida.
1873. HBS moves into the Nook Farm house in Hartford.
1878. *Poganuc People* is published.
1896. Dies on July 1, in the Nook Farm house.

With the publication of *Uncle Tom's Cabin* in 1852, Harriet Beecher Stowe became the most famous, well-paid, and widely-read American writer in the world. By the end of that year, a million and a half copies had been sold in Great Britain and its colonies alone. From then on, Stowe became the main support of her family, producing thirty books between 1852 and 1878.

Wealth and fame made her life more comfortable and glamorous than it had been during the years she and her husband supported themselves and their seven children on his low professor's salary and the fees from occasional sales of her stories. But fame and money had not essentially changed her. She was still wryly modest and energetic.

In 1873, after an unsuccessful and uncharacteristic try at high-living in an elaborate Italianate-Tudor mansion in Hartford, which had cost her a fortune to build and keep up, Stowe and her husband, Calvin, moved into a moderate-sized, Gothic-cottage-style house at Nook Farm, a community of wealthy, prominent people connected to the arts. The Stowes were drawn to the simplicity and countrified design of the architecture. This house of medium-size rooms, four below and three above, light-filled bay windows, and trellised porches, was the right setting for her modestly proportioned domestic life, of which, after the 1870s, writing formed a smaller and smaller part. Her houses and gardens were as important to her as her writing.

Stowe never thought of herself as a great artist. In writing *Uncle Tom's Cabin*, she believed that she only put down what came to her in God-sent visions. After this novel, she went ahead with her writing in a business-like way, as she had when she was a young housewife, trying to earn money with her stories. She claimed no special rights of genius, nor did she expect the return of divine inspiration.

In the Nook Farm house, Harriet Beecher Stowe chose a small single-windowed room for her study. Joined to her bedroom by a connecting door, it had originally been intended for a dressing room. Surrounded by the watercolors she had done of plants and flowers, Stowe closed herself up for at least three hours a day, writing quickly with little break in concentration. In 1878, she finished her last novel, *Poganuc People*, a realistic account of the country life she had known as a young girl growing up in Connecticut.

Through their long married life, Calvin encouraged his wife, enjoying her success, even when she earned far more than he. While she was away in New York arranging for the publication of her first book, he wrote and advised her, "[G]et a good stock of health and brush up your mind, drop the E. [her middle initial] out of your name, which only incumbers it and stops the flow and euphony, and write yourself fully and always Harriet Beecher Stowe, which is a name euphonious, flowing and full of meaning."

By the time they moved to their Nook Farm house, Calvin was no longer a teacher of biblical studies, a position he had held at Bowdoin and also at Andover Theological Seminary. In 1867, he published his only work, *The Origin and History of the Books of the Bible*, which sold well, earning him $10,000. For years, he had been chronically unable to finish this book, which was completed only with Harriet's urging and scheming. He was content to have her remain the principal writer in the family.

The Stowes made a good pair. Although they were both prone to depression, they were hardly ever depressed at the same time, and by turns, could offer each other support and encouragement. They were both articulate. Years of religious soul-searching had equipped them with powers of self-analysis and the honesty to openly discuss intimate problems. Before they moved to Nook Farm, Stowe complained that after a separation, her husband was full of ardor and affection, but he cooled to indifference after a week or two. She wanted affection that wasn't always directly connected to sex and wished that his concern for her would continue even after his desires had been fulfilled. They suffered from a lack of money and the burden of repeated pregnancies. She had twin girls and was pregnant with her third child after fifteen months of marriage. Their only method of birth control was abstinence, often enforced by long separations when one of them would take a cure at a health spa. Every passionate reunion was followed by a pregnancy. By the time they moved to the Nook Farm house they were both in their sixties. They took separate bedrooms. A domestic serenity untroubled by the fear of pregnancy may have compensated her for the loss of ardor. Stowe was no longer burdened by childcare and the heavy work of house-keeping. In her new home, she was glad to be free of the "dark side of domestic life," when she had been "sick of the smell of sour milk, and sour meat and sour everything."

At Nook Farm, she incorporated the ideas of cleanliness and organization which she and her sister Catherine had described in *The American Woman's Home,* the most important nine-teenth-century American book on household management. Instead of the usual late-Victorian arrangement of heavy drapes over curtains, she left the windows bare, lightly screening them with hoya, ferns, and trailing ivy. In a time which favored dark interiors, her rooms were exceptionally bright. For cleanliness and simplicity, she chose rush matting for the bedrooms instead of heavy difficult-to-clean carpets. The kitchen was organized to save labor: opposite the stove, a large center work-island, which contained clearly labeled storage bins for staples such as flour and sugar.

However, not all her arrangements were practical and util-itarian. Stowe had a taste for beauty, which had been sup-pressed in childhood, but which she regained on her frequent trips to Europe, where the paintings, statues, and architecture delighted her. She was thankful that the starvation of the senses she had experienced growing up in New England had not destroyed her youthful love of beauty, as she feared it might. Reacting against her strict Puritan upbringing, she satisfied her taste for beauty with a few extravagant touches: china with her own design of violets, and at Christmas, a decorated tree, still unusual in Protestant homes. In the bright light of her bare Nook Farm parlor window, she placed a reproduction of the Venus de Milo. In the garden, she was lavish, planting crocuses, snowdrops, tulips, daffodils, Canter-bury bells, chrysanthemums, delphinium, foxglove, larkspur, morning glories, sweet peas, and wild flowers like bloodroot and jack-in-the-pulpit. There were also roses, rhododendron, azaleas, lilacs, and dogwood. She spent the cold months in Florida where she sketched and painted the lush magnolias, returning to Nook Farm for the warm months when she could again work in her garden.

Along side her own paintings, she hung the oil reproductions she had brought from abroad. During one of her visits to Italy, she bought a brightly colored depiction of the Madonna for her New England parlor. Orphaned at four, and brought up in an "uncaressing, let-alone system," Stowe turned in later years from the harsh God of the Calvinist Puritans to the forgiving approachable Madonna. In her book, *Women of Sacred History* she wrote that she believed in virgin birth because Jesus as the exclusive child of a woman could feel a sympathy with a woman that no other man could feel. She wondered if her ancestors' harsh theology would have survived if they had landed in Florida instead of Plymouth Rock.

During the Nook Farm period, she was still much involved with the lives of her grown children. She gave them her immoderate and passionate devotion. Without despairing, she stood by her children when they were in trouble. Her daughter Georgiana, who became addicted to morphine, given to her to relieve a post-partum depression, died at forty-four from an overdose. Stowe lost three other children: an infant boy to cholera; her first son, Henry, in a drowning accident when he was at Dartmouth; and another son, Frederick, who was an alcoholic before he was seventeen and whom she never stopped trying to help until his mysterious disappearance in 1871. Of seven children, three survived, the twins, Eliza and Harriet, who never married, and her youngest son Charles, who continued the Beecher tradition by becoming a minister.

Stowe was drawn to seances as a means to reach her dead children. Seated in a circle in the darkened parlors of Hartford, she waited for the medium to bring her a message from the afterworld.

As she grew older, outliving five children and her husband, who died in 1886, her powers began to fail. She stopped writing and sometimes would leave her house to pick wildflowers, forgetting to return. Her neighbors, including Mark Twain, would often find her wandering around inside their houses. Often, she'd mistake men in uniform for her lost son Frederick, who had fought in the Civil War. Yet even in her decline, Harriet Beecher Stowe gave an astonishingly lucid account of herself: From Nook Farm she wrote to Oliver Wendell Holmes:

> My mental condition might be called nomadic...I wander at will from one subject to another. In pleasant summer weather I am out of doors most of my time, rambling about the neighborhood, calling upon my friends... Now and then I dip into a book much as a humming-bird, poised in air on whirring wing, darts into the heart of a flower, now here, now there, and away. Pictures delight me and afford me infinite diversion. Of *music* I am also very fond...And now I rest me, like a moored boat, rising and falling on the water, with loosened cordage and flapping sail.

She died in the Nook Farm House on July 1, 1896.

In 1924, Katharine Seymour Day, a grandniece of Harriet Beecher Stowe, bought and then lived in the Stowe house, which was drastically modernized in the 1920s. However, Day's collection of Stowe and Beecher memorabilia, papers and belongings, facilitated accurate reconstruction.

Monte Cristo Cottage
New London, Connecticut

Eugene O'Neill

Eugene O'Neill

325 Pequot Avenue
New London, Connecticut 06320
203-443-0051
203-443-5378

Open year round. 1 pm-4 pm, Monday through Friday, and by appointment. Closed on major holidays. The house occasionally is closed for
restoration—call ahead. Admission — Adults, $2.00; Children, $.50. On-
street parking on Pequot Avenue. Monte Cristo Cottage is the setting for
O'Neill's play, *Long Day's Journey into Night*. Excellent fifteen-minute
audio/visual presentation is shown at the cottage. Call ahead for information on tours, special events, and exhibitions.

1888. Born October 16, New York City to Ella Quinlan O'Neill and James
O'Neill.
**1895. EO lives at a Catholic boarding school in the Bronx
and spends his summers in New London at Monte Cristo
Cottage.**
1903. EO enters Betts Academy in Stamford.
**1906. EO leaves Princeton before completing his freshman
year.**
**1909. EO marries Kathleen Jenkins, October 2, though he
never lives with her. EO sails for Honduras. His son,
Eugene O'Neill, Jr., is born on May 5.**
1910. EO signs on a Norwegian ship as an ordinary seaman. For the next
two years, he lives a drunken life in Buenos Aires, Liverpool, and New
York.
1911. EO attempts suicide in New York.
**1912. EO returns to his family in New London. He works as a
reporter, becomes ill with tuberculosis, and enters a
sanitarium. Begins writing seriously.**
1913. EO returns to Monte Cristo Cottage, cured.
**1914. In the fall, EO leaves to take playwriting course at
Harvard.**
1916. *Bound East for Cardiff* produced in Provincetown, Massachusetts.
1920. EO wins first Pulitzer Prize for *Beyond the Horizon*. His father dies.
1928. EO leaves his second wife, Agnes Boulton, for Carlotta Monterey,
with whom he lives for the rest of his life.
1936. EO is awarded the Nobel Prize for Literature.
1939. EO completes *The Iceman Cometh*.
1943. EO is forced to give up writing because of a paralyzing disease.
1953. November 27, dies in the Shelton Hotel in Boston.
1956. *Long Day's Journey into Night*, completed in 1941, is performed for
first time.

In 1884, Eugene O'Neill's father, James O'Neill, a famous actor, bought Monte Cristo Cottage, a small, early-nineteeth-century house on Pequot Avenue overlooking the Thames River. Two years later, he bought the adjoining land, barn, and two smaller cottages, one of which had been an old schoolhouse.

By the late 1890s, the expansion and renovation of the original house was complete. James O'Neill had added a front porch in Victorian stick-style and a side tower room. To give the family more living space, he joined the old schoolhouse to the main house. The front and back parlors opened to the new one-room addition. In this informal room, with its original casement windows and tongue-in-groove paneling, James O'Neill displayed the momentoes of his theatrical career.

For most of his professional life, he spent the fall and winter on marathon long-distance tours with his acting company, endlessly repeating his enormously successful role as Edmund Dantes in *The Count of Monte Cristo*. His wife, Ella Quinlan O'Neill, and his children, James, Jr. and Eugene, traveled with him. During the summer, the family returned to Monte Cristo Cottage.

The O'Neills were an unhappy family. The children were deeply affected by their parents' problems. Eugene O'Neill became guilt-ridden that his birth was a burden to his parents. His mother, Ella, was addicted to morphine, and he felt irrationally responsible for her addiction and grew to despise her because she wouldn't break the habit. Daily, he watched the effects of her addiction. He knew when she was trying to cut down and when she had given in and injected herself. O'Neill's father, James, was an alcoholic and spent his evenings in the barroom. At home, he was obsessed about spending money on his family, which made Eugene feel even more guilty.

Left to himself during the summers at Monte Cristo Cottage, O'Neill found comfort in the sea. Before he learned to swim, he would sit for hours on the rocks along Harbor Pond. As he grew older, he became fascinated with the square-rigged schooners which jammed the harbor and, although shy and introverted with most other people, made friends with the men who crewed the ships.

In his teens, O'Neill, like his father, discovered that alcohol gave him courage and alleviated his shyness. By the time he was seventeen, he was familiar with the brothels of New

London and spent his evenings talking, drinking, and playing cards.

His excessive drinking made it impossible for him to live a responsible life. Each of his forays into the world ended with failure. He flunked out of Princeton, having spent most of his freshman year drinking, and returned to Monte Cristo Cottage. To give him something to do, his father created a job for him in the acting company. Hating his dependence on his father, he signed on a commercial, square-rigged schooner as an able-bodied seaman. The order, control, and sobriety of ship life contained him. The sea carried him out of his unhappy personal history, and for the first time in his life, he felt strong.

However, off ship, he sank into the alcoholic life of waterfront dives and flophouses. In New York in 1911, waiting until his father was in town and reasonably sure he would be rescued by friends, he tried to kill himself by taking Veronal, a barbiturate. His father brought him back to Monte Cristo Cottage and got him a job as a reporter on the New London *Telegraph.*

Writing poetry and half-heartedly working as a reporter, O'Neill seemed to be biding his time. His self-containment infuriated his fellow reporters. He sat in a corner of the city room smoking and dreaming while they did all the work. Some reporters mistakenly believed that O'Neill's father was actually paying his son's salary through an arrangement with the publisher.

Cycling to work in New London in October of 1912, O'Neill was caught in a soaking rain. He came down with a cold which left him with a dry cough, fever, and night sweats. He became weak and bedridden. By November, he had pleurisy and had to be cared for by an around-the-clock nurse. His pleurisy developed into tuberculosis. Although he was able to sit up, writing and sketching when his fever subsided, his doctors recommended a sanitarium. Convinced that his son would die, James O'Neill decided to save money by sending Eugene to a state hospital. Before O'Neill left Monte Cristo Cottage, his father had the best tailor in New London come to the house to measure him for an expensive overcoat and funeral suit.

O'Neill lasted two days at the primitive hospital. Fighting for a chance to live, he convinced his father to send him to Gaylord Farm, a private sanitarium which had achieved success with tuberculosis patients.

O'Neill returned to Monte Cristo Cottage sober and cured of tuberculosis in the spring of 1913. The death he survived inspired his writing, and the powers he discovered in surviving temporarily freed him from his father. In the spring and summer, he rested, ate well, and worked out ideas for plays.

When his parents closed Monte Cristo Cottage for the winter, he boarded at a neighbor's house across the street. This well-run, cheerful household, presided over by an easygoing, well-organized, sober couple, gave O'Neill the nourishing order he needed in which to write. Between September of 1913 and March 1914, in his room directly across the street from the empty, closed-up Monte Cristo Cottage, he completed one full-length and six one-act plays.

In the spring of 1914, when the O'Neills were in residence again, he moved back to his old room in Monte Cristo Cottage and completed *Children of the Sea*, which was later produced as *Bound East for Cardiff*. Encouraged by the young playwright's output, James O'Neill financed the publication of *Thirst And Other One-Act Plays*, Eugene O'Neill's first book.

With his family at Monte Cristo Cottage in May of 1917, he regressed, drinking heavily and bitterly attacking his father with past resentments until his father asked him to leave.

Before he stopped drinking altogether in the late twenties, O'Neill's life alternated between alcoholic binges and active, orderly sobriety in which writing was part of his cure. His parents, with whom he was in touch, lived long enough to see his great success. He made peace with his father and visited him daily when the old man was dying in a New London Hospital. James kept the telegram announcing Eugene's Pulitzer Prize on his bedside table. After having been a strong man to his son all his life, James confessed his sense of failure as an actor, and Eugene, watching his father waste away, forgave him.

After her husband's death in 1920, Ella O'Neill gave up morphine for good and sold Monte Cristo Cottage.

In 1931, Eugene O'Neill and his third wife, Carlotta, returned to New London. Pequot Avenue had been built up, and at first he couldn't find the house. When he did, it seemed small and shrunken. The sense of change overwhelmed him, and he was sorry he had come. It was his last visit.

In *Long Day's Journey Into Night* written in 1941, O'Neill returned to Monte Cristo Cottage in memory and imagination. The play is set entirely in the schoolhouse addition of the cottage and the characters are based on his family as they were in the year of 1912, when he returned to Monte Cristo Cottage after attempting suicide.

In 1937, the bank, which bought Monte Cristo Cottage from Ella O'Neill in 1920, sold the house to a real estate company. The White family lived there until the early seventies. At that time, The Eugene O'Neill Memorial Theater Center bought the house and opened it to the public.

Massachusetts

The Mount
Lenox, Massachusetts

Edith Wharton

Edith Wharton

Plunkett Street (Off Route 7 & 7A)
Lenox, Massachusetts 01240
413-637-1899

Open Mid-June-Labor Day; 12 noon-4 pm, Wednesday, Thursday, and Friday; 10 am-4 pm, Saturday, Sunday, and holiday Mondays. Open Labor Day-Mid-October; 10 am-4 pm, Saturday, Sunday, and holiday Mondays. Admission—Senior Citizens, $2.00; Adults, $3.00; Children 12-18, $2.00; Children under 12, no charge. Tours. Entrance gate 30 feet east of southern junction of routes 7 and 7A. The Mount is not visible from the road. Gatehouse and stable on the left of the long driveway which leads to the house and parking. Ask directions to the small cemetery in back of the house where Wharton's beloved dogs are buried. Productions of resident theater group, Shakespeare and Co., "Edith Wharton, Songs from the Heart." Phone ahead for information on special events.

1862. Born January 24, New York City, to George Frederic Jones and
      Lucretia Rhinelander Jones, both from old New York families.
1865. EW lives in Europe with her family until 1871.
1878. EW's first book, a collection of poems, is privately printed.
1885. EW marries Edward Robbins Wharton.
1897. *The Decoration of Houses*, written with Ogden Codman, published.
1899. The Whartons sell Land's End, their Newport house, and buy land in
      Lenox, Massachusetts. EW's first collection of short stories published.
**1902. *The Valley of Decision*, EW's first novel, published. EW
      moves into her new home, The Mount, in Lenox.**
1905. *The House of Mirth* published. Becomes a best-seller.
1907. EW begins romance with Morton Fullerton.
1911. The Mount is sold.
1913. EW divorces Teddy Wharton, moves to France where she will live
      for the rest of her life.
1916. EW is made a Chevalier of the Legion of Honor for her work for war
      refugees.
1920. EW wins Pulitzer Prize for *The Age of Innocence*.
1923. EW's only trip to America after the war.
1937. Dies August 11, at her home in St. Brice.

Edith Wharton visited Lenox in 1899 and, two years later, bought 113 acres on the southwestern edge of town for $40,600. From the land's highest point, it sloped through meadows and woods to the shore of Laurel Lake. With the income from various trust funds and an inheritance of $500,000, Edith Wharton was free to create a magnificent house. Professional success gave her confidence. Like her writing, The Mount was her creation. She chose the site, design, and decoration.

At first, she hired Ogden Codman as architect, but finding his fees for the preliminary drawings outrageous, she replaced him with Francis V.L. Hoppin, who retained most of Ogden's plans. With Belton House in Lincolnshire, England as its model, The Mount revived eighteenth-century Georgian architecture in early twentieth-century America.

The house, especially the sharply incised rows of windows in the east facade, is geometrically severe; the interior decoration is pastoral, romantic, rococo, an aristocrat's dream of country pleasure, remote from the wildness of provincial America. In the entrance hall, opposite the door, Wharton placed a bronze statue of Pan, the god of forests, pastures, and shepherds. For the upstairs rooms, she chose paintings of ladies and gentlemen in sylvan glades and of fat-winged cherubs surrounded by flowers and perfect, ripe fruit.

The layout is unusual for an American home. The main entrance on the east side, which faces away from the lake, leads into a small, rectangular, ground-floor hall. The three easy shallow steps, the narrow double doors with their polished silver pulls, and the small grotto-like room are a surprisingly unintimidating yet sophisticated introduction to a great house.

On a hot day, the entrance hall is pleasantly cool. Along the back wall are mirrored windows, which reflect the views from the clear glass windows on the front exterior wall. Behind the mirrored windows, are the large laundry room, kitchen, pantries, and servants' dining room. There is absolutely no view into the house from the entrance hall. All the grand living rooms are on the floors above, out of sight.

To the right of the entrance hall, stairs lead up to the main living floor, where a fifty-four-foot, barrel-vaulted gallery connects to the dining room, salon, and library. Straight ahead, at the end of the gallery, on the northeast corner of the house, are doors which lead to the writing room used by Edith Wharton's secretary.

The Whartons moved in in 1902 and entertained steadily during their summer and fall stays. Guests were greeted with iced champagne to refresh them after the long train ride up from New York. Then a servant would show them to their rooms. There are four guest rooms on the second floor. The multiple entrances of the rooms on the main living floor were designed so that Wharton and her guests could be private yet have many choices for movement. The library, salon, and dining room open onto the terrace. These light-filled rooms also connected to the gallery and to each other, so it is possible to walk from the dining room, at one end, to the library at the other, and from the library into the writing room, or to weave and circle in and out of the gallery to any of the other rooms. The design of the house is grand, but the rooms are not enormous. Edith Wharton succeeded in creating an architecturally important, yet intimate, setting for her life.

She ran the house the way a director might stage a play. Servants were an important part of her domestic enterprise. She communicated her enthusiasm to them, and they became inspired workers. She provided legacies for their retirement and housed them well. In addition to the two people who supervised the staff, there were Wharton's personal maid, housemaids, footmen, cook, kitchen helpers, a gardener and his staff, and a chauffeur.

Wharton had a suite of rooms—boudoir, bath, and bedroom—at the far end of the second-floor corridor, next to the servants' stairs and the servants' wing. She only had to press the top buzzer marked "HOUSEMAID" or the bottom one marked "SVTS HALL" and the maid would quickly appear.

From the windows of her bedroom, she saw perfect gardens, which contrasted with wild woods and distant water. Her boudoir/sitting room looked out over the circular, pebble-lined entrance court, so she could hear and see every arrival and departure. She inhabited a house and a world she had created for her artistic pleasure. She had a small, rectangular mirror cut to fit a low panel of her boudoir wall, so, alone or with her guests, she could see herself sitting in front of the fireplace. Standing, she saw only her feet; seated, she occupied the entire field, as if she were arranged in an informal portrait—life turned into art.

Wharton kept to a strict writing schedule. After breakfast, she wrote in bed, tossing the filled pages to the floor for the maid to collect just before lunchtime. Her secretary, Anna Bahlman, who lived at The Mount when the Whartons were in residence, would type the pages and return them by the following morning, ready for corrections. In these morning hours, alone in her bed at The Mount, Wharton completed, *The House of Mirth, The Age of Innocence, Summer, Madame de Treymes,* and parts of *Ethan Frome.*

Teddy never disturbed her. He slept alone in a room separated from his wife's by two sets of doors and a dressing room. Teddy helped run the house. He had a talent for detail and arrangement. A considerate and charming host, he loved to serve guests his rare and exquisite wines.

From the outside, Edith Wharton's life seemed successful. She was wealthy in her own right and became a best-selling author with *The House of Mirth.* But she had never felt loved. She was still like the character of a short story she had written in 1891: an unhappily married woman, whose nature was like a grand house, social in the public rooms, conventional in the family rooms, but whose real self, stripped of pretense, waited alone behind a closed door in a remote wing of the house for someone who never came.

By her mid-forties, she realized she had poured all of her energy into work and had closed herself off to love. Since the earliest days of her marriage, she had mistakenly believed she was incapable of feeling sexual pleasure. Sensitive, vulnerable, and totally ignorant about sex, she had been shocked and frightened on her wedding night. Teddy felt guilty for having violated her. After repeated tries and then a painful consummation during their honeymoon, she and Teddy had no sex at all for the rest of their marriage.

Nevertheless, their marriage might have lasted, if Edith Wharton's sexuality had stayed frozen. Her accomplishments

went stale; her life became arid, her need for order, mechanical
and driven. Realizing her life was half over, she was afraid she
would die without ever having loved. She wanted a full relationship with a man, but she chose not to turn to Teddy. At the
age of forty-five, she fell in love with Morton Fullerton.

Wharton had met him briefly in Paris in 1906. Fullerton,
following Henry James's urging, then visited Wharton at The
Mount late in October, the following year. They went out
driving and it began to snow. While the chauffeur put chains
on the car wheels, Wharton picked yellow witch hazel. She and
Fullerton saw meaning in her finding this late-blooming
flower. When Fullerton left, he enclosed a sprig in his note
of thanks.

Fullerton, unlike Wharton, had a long erotic history. He
had been the lover of both men and women. At forty-two, he
looked young. He was the type of man many fell in love
with—somewhat passive, an object of desire.

Soon after Fullerton left, Wharton began a journal which
became a long letter to him. They became lovers in Paris in the
spring of 1908. When she returned to The Mount in the spring,
she abandoned her usual well-organized writing schedule.
Instead she wrote poems to Fullerton, whom she continued to
see during her winter visits abroad.

When Edith Wharton became Morton Fullerton's lover,
Teddy Wharton fell apart. He went through one severe breakdown after another, and in an act of revenge, embezzled
$500,000 from his wife's estate, which he managed as cotrus-
tee. Once she discovered the loss, Wharton refused to allow
him to take care of her financial affairs. Removed from his
only real job, he felt even more unmanned.

In the summer of 1911, in act of conscience and duty,
Wharton left Paris and joined her husband at The Mount. It
was the first time she had been to Lenox in almost two years.
For part of that time, Teddy had been a patient in a Swiss
sanitarium. Henry James, a frequent guest at The Mount,
arrived in Lenox before Teddy. James advised Wharton to sell
the house and divorce her husband. Still acting on her sense of
duty, Wharton offered to live with Teddy at The Mount during
the summer and allow him to manage the house on a fixed

allowance, if he would resign as cotrustee of her estate. He refused. In September, giving Teddy authority to sell The Mount, Edith Wharton returned to Europe, where she lived for the rest of her life.

The Mount passed through private owners until 1949, when it was used by Foxhollow School for Girls. In 1972, it was put on the National Register of Historic Buildings. Shakespeare and Company, a private acting group, has performed at The Mount since 1978. In 1980, The National Trust for Historic Preservation bought The Mount and resold it to Edith Wharton Restoration.

Arrowhead

Pittsfield, Massachusetts

Herman Melville

Herman Melville

780 Holmes Road
Pittsfield, Massachusetts 01201
413-442-1793

Open June 1-October 31, 10 am-5 pm, Monday through Saturday; 1 pm-5 pm, Sunday. Last tour at 4:15 pm. November 1-May 31, open to groups by appointment. Admission—Adults, $2.00; Students, $1.00; Senior Citizens, $1.50. Parking in large lot behind house. Faithful restoration of study where Melville wrote *Moby-Dick*. Photographs, books, furniture belonging to the Melvilles, as well as bequests of eighteenth- and nineteenth-century furniture to the Berkshire Historical Society. Self-guided nature walk. Restored barn. Arrowhead Shop open all year round.

1819. August 1, born in New York City to Allan Melville and Maria Gansevoort Melville.
1830. HM enters Albany Academy.
1832. HM's father dies. HM withdraws from Albany Academy.
1839. HM joins crew of the *St. Lawrence*, sails to Liverpool. In Fall, after return, HM begins teaching school.
1840. In December, HM signs on the whaler, *Acushnet*, for Pacific voyage.
1842. HM deserts ship in the Marquesas Islands and lives in Tahiti. Signs on Nantucket whaler.
1843. HM discharged from whaler in the Hawaiian Islands, works in Honolulu. HM becomes an ordinary seaman on the American frigate *United States* and sails home.
1846. English publication of Melville's first book, *Narrative of a Four Months' Residence among the Natives of a Valley of the Marquesas Islands*, published in America in March as *Typee*.
1847. August 4, HM marries Elizabeth Shaw in Boston. They live in New York with Melville's brother Allan, and Allan's wife, Sophia.
1849. Malcolm, their first child, is born. HM finishes *Redburn*, his fourth book. HM sails to England to meet his publishers.
1850. HM meets Hawthorne in the Berkshires and buys farm in Pittsfield.
1851. Second child, Stanwix, born. *Moby-Dick* published.
1856. *The Piazza Tales* is published. *The Confidence Man* is finished. HM sails to Europe and the Mediterranean.
1863. HM sells his farm, Arrowhead, and moves to New York.
1867. Malcolm Melville commits suicide.
1885. HM resigns as Inspector of Customs for the Port of New York.
1891. HM finishes *Billy Budd*, dies on September 28 in New York.

Herman Melville and his wife, Elizabeth Shaw Melville, and their first child, Malcolm, spent part of July and August of 1850 in Pittsfield at the Berkshire home of Melville's widowed aunt, where Melville had spent many childhood vacations. In early September, Melville bought the adjoining 150-acre farm with a $3000 loan from his father-in-law, Lemuel Shaw, The Chief Justice of the Superior Court of Massachusetts.

There were apple orchards on the south side of the house, hayfields on the north, and in back, to the west, a pasture which ended at a woodlot. While plowing the fields for the first time, Melville turned up Indian arrowheads, and called his new home, Arrowhead.

He had an amateur's love of outdoor work. Although he planned to earn a living by a combination of writing and farming, he managed to raise only enough feed for his horse and cow, and vegetables for his own table. Elizabeth Melville was unable to help him run the farm. She had been raised in a well-to-do family, where servants did the work, and she never developed a talent for housekeeping.

Melville's mother and four unmarried sisters moved in and took over the household work. His mother was a good manager. His sisters adored him and believed in his writing, particularly Augusta and Helen, who worked as his copyists. His mother's presence was a problem, however, her management too efficient and overbearing.

The eighteenth-century house, shared by this largely female family, had originally been an inn on the coach route between Hartford, Connecticut and Bennington, Vermont. The fireplace according to Melville, swallowed "cords of wood as a whale does boats." The enormous center chimney was forty-eight feet in circumference at the base, and sixteen feet at the roof. Melville joked that the chimney was the main structure and the house an annex. Between the two front parlors, which backed up to the kitchen, the stairs rose from a small front hall, like scaffolding against the gigantic chimney, holding cupboards and closets, which Melville described as "nests in the crotches of some old oak."

By the time he bought Arrowhead, Melville was already

famous for South-Sea adventure novels based on his own experience. However, when he began *Moby-Dick* soon after he moved in, he could not force himself to produce another adventure story, even though he still owed his publisher $700 for advances against royalties which hadn't been earned. He was worried about money, but decided to abandon the popular market and write according to his own standards of greatness. Even before he finished *Moby-Dick*, he thought of himself as a martyr crucified by popular taste, and, in a letter, claimed to a friend, "Tho' I wrote the Gospels in this century, I should die in the gutter."

Beginning at the end of August 1850, Melville followed a daily routine which varied little for almost a year. He was up at eight, fed the horse, cut up pumpkins for the cow, had his breakfast in the kitchen, and then went up the back stairs to his second-floor study. From his desk he could see the double ridges of Mount Greylock. After he got the fire going in the small fireplace behind him, using a single harpoon for a poker, he would spread out his manuscript and work without interruption until 2:30, when his wife or one of his sisters would knock on the door. He would join them for dinner, return to work, and later go to the village for mail and supplies.

Moby-Dick absorbed his life and changed his perception of the landscape. By December, when the ground was covered with snow, he wrote that he woke up with a "sea-feeling...I look out my window in the morning when I rise as I would out of a port-hole of a ship in the Atlantic. My room seems a ship's cabin; & at nights when I wake up & hear the wind shrieking, I almost fancy there is too much sail on the house." Some days he would ignore his sister's or his wife's knock, write all day without eating, and ride to the village in the dark. He finished *Moby-Dick* in a rented room in New York, where he went in the summer of 1851 to be away from the distractions of farm work.

Despite this year of hard labor, Melville felt a tremendous rush of energy when he completed *Moby-Dick*. Nathaniel Hawthorne, Melville's closest friend, who lived nearby, was one of the few people, at that time, who understood the novel.

Hawthorne wrote a praising letter, which elicited Melville's soaring reply, "A sense of unspeakable security is in me this moment, on account of your having understood the book."

Just after he completed *Moby-Dick*, Melville was the energetic center of an all-night camping party on Mount Greylock. He climbed trees, cut wood for the fire, and told story after story. In his vigorous bearing, it was easy to see the man who had lived with natives in the South Seas, shipped out on a whaler, and come home on an American frigate where he was flogged and put into irons for refusing to shave off his beard.

His publisher, critics, and public had wanted more adventure stories from the man who had lived with cannibals. But Melville had wanted to write the Great American Novel.

After *Moby-Dick* was published in 1851, Melville's popularity rapidly declined, but he didn't fully realize the extent of the decline until the critics ripped apart *Pierre,* published the following year. They criticized Melville for having a diseased mind. Melville could not, as he had after finishing *Moby Dick,* compulsively throw himself into work. He lost confidence in himself. The strain showed. He was depressed and exhausted. His family thought he was going mad. His bitterness repelled his friends, and Hawthorne, the one friend who might have helped, had moved away.

Making use of Hawthorne's friendship with President Pierce, Melville tried unsuccessfully to obtain a consulship in the South Seas or at Antwerp. Later, he had some success on the lecture circuit, but writing was the only profession he knew. Between 1853 and 1856, he finished five books. In warm weather, he set up a desk on the shaded north porch, which he had built in 1851. There, he felt sheltered but not shut in.

Deferring and encouraging, his family was careful not to disturb him. His wife had always supported his work. In the early years of their marriage, Melville would read Elizabeth what he had written that day. Although she wasn't literary, she gave him the encouragement he needed. Later, children and money problems strained their marriage. Yet, Elizabeth protected him, particularly after the failure of *Moby-Dick*. She even wrote to people that he was "morbidly sensitive" to imagined slights and urged them to treat him carefully. Eventually, she managed their finances, because, as she wrote, Melville's "studious habits and tastes" disinclined him for the job. In later years, she acted as his agent. Elizabeth became more and more practical as her husband retreated.

Although Melville felt the feminine and masculine spheres of the house were opposed, describing the women as constitutionally liberal, bustling, changing, cleaning, improving, full of plans to remove the sacred old chimney, and himself the conservator of the masculine, dusty and ancient, it was the women who kept Arrowhead going and who supported Melville in his worst time.

Melville also had the help of his father-in-law, Judge Shaw, who came through with generous gifts of money and long-term loans, which he never collected. Shaw had money and enjoyed spending it. He gave so easily, Melville never felt oppressively beholden, but it must have been clear that Elizabeth felt protected by her father, not her husband. She spent months in his house in Boston, where she gave birth to three of her children, Stanwix, Elizabeth, and Frances.

The Melvilles had four children in all. Malcolm, the eldest, was born the year before they moved to Pittsfield. Because he was the protected child of the house, there was no room for his own children. They lived under the strain of their father's great work. He expected complete obedience. His constant fault finding and corrosive sarcasm had their effect. Malcolm killed himself at eighteen, making sure his father would find the body. At eighteen, Stanwix ran away to sea.

Melville had been tired of the country for years. In 1856, he sold off 80 acres of the farm, and, the following year, he put the house up for sale. Three years later, he turned over the deed to Judge Shaw for payment of his debts. Shaw, who died in 1860, cancelled Melville's debts and left Arrowhead to Elizabeth. Melville finally sold the house to his brother Allan, in partial payment for a house which Allan owned in New York. In 1863, after Arrowhead was sold, the Melvilles left Pittsfield to move to their new house in New York.

Melville didn't get away from Arrowhead easily. On moving day, the loaded wagon he was driving turned over, and he spent weeks at a neighbor's house convalescing from a dislocated shoulder and broken ribs. Whatever their disappointments at Arrowhead, Elizabeth wrote that she mostly remembered the fresh "reviving air."

In New York, Melville settled into an obscure life as Inspector of Customs with the Port of New York, one of the lowest political appointments available. With age came self-acceptance. He saw himself as a man out of joint with the times. He wrote more poetry and drew closer to Elizabeth. She encouraged him to retire from the custom's job after she inherited a legacy from her brother. Renewed by a voyage to Cuba, Melville began *Billy Budd* in 1888.

Allan Melville left the house to his daughter. Arrowhead remained in the family until 1927, after which it passed through a number of private owners, until it was bought by the Berkshire County Historical Society in 1975.

The
William Cullen Bryant
House

Cummington, Massachusetts

William Cullen Bryant

William Cullen Bryant

Photo courtesy of The William Cullen Bryant Homestead,
a property of The Trustees of Reservations.

Bryant Road (off Route 112)
Cummington, Massachusetts 01026
413-634-2244

Open last week in June-Labor Day, Fridays, Saturdays, Sundays and holidays, 1-5; Labor Day-Columbus Day, Saturday and Sunday, 1-5. Admission—Adults, $2.00; Children, under 12, $1.00. Parking on drive near
house. Beautiful setting overlooking Cummington hills, almost two
hundred acres of unspoiled upland farm country. Avenue of two-hundred-
year-old sugar maples. Collection of Bryant furnishings, including souve-
nirs of foreign travel.

**1794. Born November 3, in Cummington, Massachusetts, to
Sarah Snell Bryant and Peter Bryant.**
**1810. WCB enters Williams College as a sophomore, but
withdraws after first year.**
1811. WCB reads law in Worthington, Massachusetts.
1816. WCB forms law partnership in Great Barrington.
1821. WCB marries Frances Fairchild, June 11. *Poems*, his first collection,
published.
1822. Daughter Frances born, January 2.
1826. WCB becomes the assistant editor of the *Evening Post* in New York.
Becomes editor in 1829.
1831. Daughter Julia born, June 29.
1834. WCB takes first of six trips to Europe.
1843. WCB buys home in Roslyn, Long Island.
1848. WCB turns *Evening Post* into leading anti-slavery newspaper.
1866. Frances Bryant dies.
1878. June 12, dies of a stroke in New York.

In 1815, at the age of twenty-two, William Cullen Bryant left the family farm in Cummington, Massachusetts to begin practicing law. His widowed mother, unable to make a living out of the depleted soil, went into debt, and in 1835, was forced to sell the farm. She and her eldest son, Austin, then joined two other sons and a daughter, who had gone out to Illinois to farm. In 1865, eighteen years after his mother's death, Bryant, now a successful poet and well-to-do newspaper editor, bought back the homestead.

As a child, Bryant had been forced to submit to his strict-Calvinist grandfather, Squire Snell, who had settled in Cummington in 1774. Snell cleared 500 acres of first-growth timber and successfully grew rye, wheat, and maize. He made enough money from farming to build a second house in 1785, which became the family homestead.

Bryant had no freedom and little happiness during the years he lived at the homestead. Later, he was always conscious that adult pleasure—he was an avid, tireless traveler—could never make up for the youthful joy he had completely missed. Bryant had been a sickly child, first with colic, then with migraine headaches. The cures for the headaches were harsh: lancing, bleeding, and ice-cold baths.

Besides suffering from bad health and tormenting cures, Bryant grew up in complete awe and fear of adults. That children should be seen and not heard was a rule literally interpreted in the Bryant home. Adults were distant—to encourage respect. If Bryant or his brothers and sisters misbehaved in any way, their grandfather beat them with a bundle of birch rods, which hung on a nail in the kitchen as a reminder. Not only did Bryant have to submit to beatings without protest, but he periodically had to gather wood for the whip. At morning and evening prayers, Bryant was terrified by his grandfather's description of the punishments in hell. To the child the old man held the power of life and death. As Justice of the Peace in Cummington, Snell sentenced those convicted of serious crimes to death or public floggings. At home, he ruled the family.

Bryant's father was beholden to Snell. The Squire had lent him money to keep him out of debtor's prison after some bad investments. Bryant saw his father eventually pay his debts and get out from under the old man's tyranny, but he realized, during his childhood, that his parents were not in charge and could not or would not protect him from his grandfather. Although sickly, Bryant was put to work in the fields. When he didn't rake hay fast enough, the teeth of his grandfather's rake dug into his heels.

Bryant's parents were not as harsh as Grandfather Snell, but they were not affectionate. In a life given completely to child-bearing and hard work, affection must have seemed an unaffordable luxury. Sarah Bryant gave birth to seven children in fourteen years, all of whom survived into adulthood. She spun and wove cloth for all the family clothes, which she made; did all the baking, cooking, cleaning, washing, and ironing; made twine, candles, and soap; wove straw hats; raised geese and plucked their feathers for pillows and featherbeds. She fed the family on home-brewed beer, homemade cheese and sausage, and honey from the bees she tended. In 1811, when Bryant was about to leave to study law in a nearby town, Sarah Bryant cut out a coat for him on December 3 and finished it on December 7. She was a one-woman industry.

As he grew, Bryant emulated his father, a doctor who wrote poetry. His father let him read through the large library and encouraged him with praise and criticism. He was a prodigy by thirteen, writing "The Embargo," an anti-Jefferson poem which Peter Bryant brought to Boston and arranged to have published. His father also sent the early version of "Thanatopsis" to the *North American Review*. With the publication of this poem, in 1817, William Cullen Bryant became a recognized poet. His father died in 1820. When his mother sold the farm in 1835, the only thing Bryant asked to keep was his father's library of 700 books.

Bryant had become a famous poet, influential Democratic newspaper editor, advisor to presidents, and, like his father, a doctor. Wanting to share his success, he bought back his childhood home in Cummington and invited his brothers and their wives back for a long family reunion in 1866. But while his family waited for Bryant to join them, Bryant's wife, Francis, died at their home on Long Island.

Bryant finally returned to Cummington in the spring of 1868 with his daughter, Julia, after a trip to Europe and an interval of deep mourning. By then, renovations he had planned when he bought the house were complete. Bryant restored the rooms where he had been happiest. For his study he duplicated the wing his father used for medical offices, which the previous owners had removed.

Feeling no obligation to keep his grandfather's house intact, Bryant had workmen jack up the two-story main house and build a large new parlor and dining room. On the second floor, what had originally been the two front rooms of the farmhouse, became, on the southwest side, Bryant's bedroom, and on the southeast side, his daughter Julia's room. At the back of the house was a long ell, containing the old kitchen, which Bryant's servants used as a sitting room, and the large 'new' kitchen, which Bryant's father built in 1801. When he was finished, Bryant had an eighteenth-century farmhouse perched on top of a Victorian parlor. The rooms were decorated in a way Bryant's grandparents and parents could not have afforded: in the parlor, Delft fireplace tiles with finely drawn scenes; in his study and bedroom, marble fireplaces, polished like expensive French clocks, one chocolate-brown, the other sea-green.

He paid T.H. Dawes, a local man, $1,000 a year to care for the farm and supply food for the Bryants and guests. Bryant and Dawes met each April and made plans. The stone walls usually needed repair. Bryant always wanted more trees. Dawes planted a windscreen of spruce, hemlock, and pine on the northwest side of the house. On the east side, there were five sugar maples, which Bryant's father had planted, one for each son. To the already existing apple orchard, Bryant added 1,300 apple trees. He also planted 200 pear trees, a number of cherry and plum trees, and blackberry and raspberry bushes.

Already in his seventies when he moved back to Cummington, Bryant was still vigorous. After a sickly childhood, Bryant had become a health enthusiast. He was out of bed by 4:30 or 5 am and exercised in his room. He pole-vaulted across his bed, pulled himself up on a horizontal bar, and swung a light chair around his head. When he had some heavy farm work to do, he shortened his work-out. After his routine, he bathed in the new, sloping, tin tub in the second-floor bathroom, one of the first in Cummington with indoor plumbing. Breakfast was at 7 am. Bryant's diet was mostly vegetarian: for breakfast, either hominy-and-milk or oatmeal or wheat grits, usually a baked apple or some other fruit, brown bread, and sometimes hot chocolate. He worked in his study until 1 pm with a short break in the garden or the orchard. After a mid-day dinner of mostly vegetables, he hiked ten or fifteen miles a day with his brothers. The evenings were quiet, a light meal of bread and butter and fruit at seven, in bed by nine or ten.

Physical fitness was the only subject for which Bryant showed any enthusiasm. Most people who knew Bryant called him a cold man. He had grown up afraid of feeling and had not developed his emotional side. Emerson said he acted like a well-behaved child. Hawthorne understood the tragedy of his nature and observed that when Bryant's wife was seriously ill, Bryant could not feel sorrow or any other emotion and therefore the world must have always seemed remote and without substance. Bryant couldn't touch the heart of things and take hold.

He knew many people, had long associations with artists, writers, and reporters, but he had no deeply intimate friendships. At Cummington, he was at ease with his family. His unmarried daughter, Julia, served as his hostess, and his brothers, who shared his interest in botany, joined him for long summer hikes through the familiar territory of their boyhood.

Bryant missed his wife, Frances, whose more outgoing nature had compensated for his reserve. She had accepted his careful provision for his family as a sign of love: there were few caresses or endearments. Her final illness became a bond; they discussed symptoms and cures. Bryant successfully nursed her through a long, near-fatal illness in Europe in 1857. It was the most important experience of his adult life. When he was sure of her recovery, he had himself baptized into the Unitarian Church in Naples.

Never prolific, Bryant wrote even fewer poems after his wife's death. But he found an outlet for his restless energy. In the mornings, in his country study in Cummington, he slowly translated the *Odyssey*. He still remembered the Greek he had learned at fourteen, when his father had boarded him with a country minister for a dollar a week. Although steel-tipped pens were in use, Bryant still used a quill pen, which he sharpened with a jackknife. Byrant's name on the translation of the *Odyssey* insured sales, and he eventually made $20,000 on its publication. In his mid-seventies, he found himself writing poems again.

On May 29, 1878 after giving a speech in Central Park, he refused a carriage and walked to his host's house, without an umbrella to shade him from the unusually hot sun. He fell and was knocked unconscious, but after coming to in a few minutes, insisted on going to his house on West Sixteenth Street. There he died of a stroke on June 12. He was eighty-four.

Bryant left the homestead to his daughter Julia. It remained in the family until 1927, when it was acquired by the Trustees of Reservations along with an endowment from the Bryant family.

The Homestead
Amherst, Massachusetts

Emily Dickinson

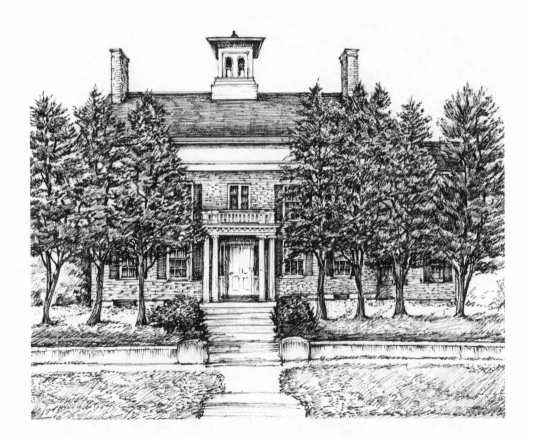

Emily Dickinson

280 Main Street
Amherst, MA 01002
413-542-2321 (Public Affairs Office of Amherst College)

Open May 1-October 1, Tuesdays and Fridays; October 2-April 31, Tuesday. Open only for tours which begin *promptly* at at 3:00, 3:45, and 4:30, and include the hall, the front and back parlors and Emily Dickinson's room. Admission—Adults, $2.00; Children under 12, no charge. The varied garden is planted with bulbs, flowering shrubs, perennials and wild flowers familiar to Emily Dickinson and common to nineteenth-century gardens. The white oak, the pear tree, the hemlocks which border the drive and the path to the Evergreens, and the front hedge of hemlock survive from the original plantings.

1830. Born December 10 in the Homestead in Amherst, Massachusetts to Emily Norcross Dickinson and Edward Dickinson and lives in the Homestead until 1840.
1847. ED finishes seventh year at Amherst Academy; enters Mount Holyoke.
1848. After her first year, ED withdraws from Mount Holyoke.
1850. Amherst College *Indicator* publishes ED's Valentine poem.
1855. ED goes to Washington, in February, to visit her father, a Representative to Congress. November, ED moves into the Homestead with family.
1856. ED's brother, Austin, and Susan Gilbert marry and move into the Evergreens next door to the Homestead.
1862. ED writes more than 300 poems and begins correspondence with Thomas Higginson, an editor.
1864. ED spends seven months in Cambridgeport, Massachusetts while having eye treatments in Boston.
1874. ED's father dies in Boston, June 16.
1882. Mother dies, November 14 at the Homestead.
1883. Nephew Gilbert dies on September 8, at the Evergreens. ED becomes ill.
1886. Dies on May 15 at the Homestead.
1955. ED's complete poems finally published.

The Homestead was at the center of all the Dickinsons' lives. It was their security and sign of their preeminent position in Amherst. Emily Dickinson's grandfather, Samuel Dickinson, built the Homestead in 1813 and built it to last. The square, solid, impressive, Federal mansion was the town's first brick building.

Emily Dickinson was born in the Homestead in 1830. That year, her grandfather, Samuel, sold the east half of the Homestead to her father, Edward, for $1,500. In 1833, near bankruptcy, Samuel Dickinson sold the west half of the house to General Mack and left Amherst. Dickinson and her family stayed on, sharing the house with the Macks, until 1840, when her father sold the east side of the house to General Mack and the family moved to a new home in Amherst.

Edward Dickinson bought back the entire property in 1855 for $4,000, redeeming the family's reputation. He had become a successful lawyer and was now able to expand the Homestead. In 1855, he added a two-story east wing and conservatory; a back ell which housed a kitchen, washroom, and shed; a veranda; and a cupola. The new east wing contained a dining room which opened to a conservatory facing Main Street and the south. Emily's parents took the new bedroom over the dining room. The children, Austin, twenty-six, Emily, twenty-five, and Lavinia, twenty-two, each had a good sized room. Emily's corner room had two windows on the south and two windows on the west and got warm south sun and brilliant sunsets.

To the northeast of the house were the barn and icehouse; to the east, an orchard of apple, cherry, peach, pear, and plum trees, grape arbors, flowering shrubs, vegetable and flower gardens, and somewhere out back, the outhouse. Across Main Street was the Dickinson meadow of eleven-and-a-half acres. A coachman, stableman, gardener, and various helpers worked the land and groomed the prize horses.

The Dickinson men were involved in every important civic project in town, from the bringing of the railroad to Amherst to the planting of trees and shrubs. The lives of the Dickinson women were centered around home and family. Shortly after they moved back to the Homestead, Emily's mother became ill. The onset of menopause unsettled and debilitated this already anxious and timid woman. All of the household responsibilities fell on Emily and her sister, Lavinia, until their father finally hired a maid.

Even then the work was strenuous. The woodstoves had to be cleaned, filled, and lit each morning. Without indoor plumbing, water had to be carried from the well in buckets and then transferred to pitchers which were brought up to the bedrooms. Dickinson, her mother (when she was able), and the maid prepared the meals from scratch. The Dickinsons kept their own chickens, cows, and pigs. Emily Dickinson did the family baking for four adults and many guests, tending and regulating the woodstove, until she got a deep bed of coals and a steady heat. Besides bread, she baked cakes, cookies, puddings, and biscuits. Holiday baking was more complicated. Cloves and mace for fruitcake were pounded in a mortar, the nutmeg and cinnamon were grated, and the spices were added to the rest of the ingredients: pounds of flour, sugar, butter, raisins, currants, citron, molasses, brandy, and eggs—all mixed by hand. Most of the family's clothes were made at home. A dressmaker cut the patterns and Emily and Lavinia Dickinson did the finishing, long careful work of fine-stitching, triple seams, hems, button holes, and facings. Although Emily Dickinson disliked cleaning, she did her share.

Her parents were meticulous, and she and her sister, Lavinia tried to please them. However, Dickinson's seeming compliance concealed her deep anger. Once, her father complained of being given a chipped plate at dinner. She took the plate out to the garden and smashed it to pieces on a stone — so it would no longer offend him, she said.

After Dickinson completed her share of the housework and paid outward obedience to her father's rules, she had time and privacy to write. She chose her own friends, became a poet even though her Puritan father believed poetry was not a proper vocation, and never joined her father's church. She attended morning prayers in the Homestead, but she did not believe. She said, "They are religious—except me—and address an Eclipse, every morning—whom they call their 'Father.'"

Dickinson would write in the very early morning, before the family came down at dawn, after midday dinner, at night, and on Sundays, violating the Sabbath while her family was at church. She wrote in her room. The walls were thick; once she closed the heavy door, she had quiet and privacy. She also wrote in the dining room, where she could look up from a poem or letter to the conservatory crowded with flowers. She said that she had only to cross the floor of the dining room "to stand in the Spice Isles." Here without stinting she grew "crocuses...fuchsia...primoses...heliotropes by the aprons full ...jessamine...gilliflowers, magenta...mignonette...sweet alyssum bountiful, and carnation[s]." She also worked in the kitchen, writing on whatever paper she could find: brown paper bags, the backs of recipes. She wrote quickly and often for a specific occasion. She hardly seems to have ever stopped writing.

At the Homestead, her output was astonishing, almost two thousand poems. The more than one thousand surviving letters are only a fraction of those she wrote. In the thirty-one years she lived at the Homestead, in increasing seclusion from 1855, when she was twenty-five, until her death, in 1886, at fifty-five, she single-mindedly followed her genius, bravely exploring in her poems the most extreme mental states and finding that she was grateful to be herself and not someone else.

Between 1858 and 1863, she suffered mental disturbances which she called "a terror" and "a snarl in the brain." During that time, she wrote three letters to an unidentified person she called "Master." The letters exist in drafts, and it is not known if she ever sent them. In one of these letters, she called herself, "Daisy—who never flinched thro' that awful parting, but held her life so tight he should not see the wound..."

She loved her sister, Lavinia, who faced the world for her, and her dog, Carlo, but she had always felt a chilling distance between herself and her parents. There had never been any physical affection or tenderness between Dickinson and her mother until her mother's final illness. After her mother's death in 1875, Dickinson wrote, "We were never intimate Mother and children while she was our Mother—but Mines in the same Ground meet by tunneling and when she became our Child, the Affection came." But none of the Dickinson children were ever able to reach their father while he was alive. Near death, Dickinson's father said he felt that he had passed his life on an island. Patriarchal, Puritan, and locked in, he was afraid of feeling and physical passion. Dickinson's brother,

Austin, kissed his father only once—when Edward Dickinson lay in his coffin. Dickinson did not attend the service or the funeral. From then on, she never left the house and began to dress exclusively in exquisite and immaculate white.

Dickinson had felt pity for her father's isolation, but she inherited his fear of the body. Shy and ashamed, she refused to have her picture taken and refused to be fitted by dressmakers and treated by doctors. She wrote to a friend, whose husband was due back after a long trip, "Am told that fasting gives to food marvellous Aroma, but by birth a Bachelor, disavow Cuisine."

She could, however, express her feelings. With poems and letters, she reached her private audience. Only seven of Dickinson's 1,779 poems were published while she was alive. She began in 1858 to arrange the poems in groups, possibly with the thought of a future book. With darning needle and thread, she bound the poems in packets. Editors were not receptive to the individual poems she sent them. She continued to write, however, and to send poems and letters to friends, 276 poems to her sister-in-law, who lived next door and who was the inspiration for many of them. She also sent poems to Thomas Higginson, an editor of the *Atlantic Monthly*, who, although he refused to publish her, became her friend.

The few people outside the family circle she consented to meet had to come to the Homestead to see her. After Helen Hunt Jackson, a famous novelist of the time, visited in 1876, she wrote to Dickinson, "I felt like a great ox talking to a white moth, and begging it to come and eat grass with me to see if it could not turn itself into beef! How Stupid.—"

Dickinson left the Homestead only once after 1874. In October 1883 on the night of her eight-year-old nephew's death, she crossed the yard to her brother's house, which she hadn't entered in fifteen years. Dickinson saw her nephew and collapsed. Later, she wrote, "The Dyings have been too deep for me."

Dickinson died in the Homestead on May 15, 1886, at the age of fifty-five. The physician's certificate gives Bright's disease as the cause of death.

Dickinson was laid out in the hall of the Homestead in a white casket, a bunch of blue violets at her throat. Thomas Higginson read a poem of Emily Bronte's. Lavinia put two heliotropes in the coffin, which was decorated with a wreath of blue violets. There were no other flowers. Dickinson had left directions. Six of the Homestead's workmen carried her coffin out the back door, through the garden, then through the barn and across the fields in back of the house to the family plot. Dickinson had requested that they keep the coffin in sight of the house as they walked.

Going through her sister's room, Lavinia discovered poems crowded into a four-drawer, camphor-wood chest. She had not realized that her sister had written so much.

Lavinia lived on in the Homestead until her death in 1899, leaving the house to her niece, who sold it to the Parke family. Amherst College bought the Homestead in 1965 and maintains the house as a private residence, part of which they open to the public.

In 1955, Emily Dickinson's poems were finally published.

Fruitlands

Harvard, Massachusetts

Amos Bronson Alcott

Amos Bronson Alcott

Prospect Hill
Harvard, Massachusetts 01451
617-456-3924

Open May 30-September 30, 1-5 pm, Tuesday through Sunday, closed
Monday except when Monday is a holiday. Admission—Adults, $3.00;
Children 6-16, $.50; Children under 6, no charge. Purchase tickets at the
reception center. Parking on the right, in the upper lot across from the
Miriam Shaw Building and reception center, and in the middle parking
lot, at the end of the drive nearest the Fruitlands farmhouse. Tickets
admit visitors to four museums: The Picture Gallery, The American
Indian Museum, Shaker House, and Fruitlands. Restrooms in the reception center and in Prospect House, the second building on the left as you
enter the grounds. Snack bar in Prospect House, observation terrace to the
rear. There are no electric lights in the Fruitlands farmhouse: on dark
days, bring a flashlight so you can read the interesting letters on display.

1799. Born November 29, 1799 to Anna Bronson and Joseph Chatfield
Alcox in Wolcott, Connecticut.
1818. ABA becomes a peddlar in Virginia.
1823. ABA teaches school in Connecticut.
1830. ABA marries Abigail May on May 23 in Boston. *Observations on
the Principles and Methods of Infant Instruction* is published.
1831. Anna, his first child, is born in Germantown, Pennsylvania, where
he is teaching.
1832. Louisa May, ABA's second child, born in Germantown, Pennsylvania, November 29.
1834. ABA opens the Temple School in Boston.
1840. Moves with family to Concord, Massachusetts after failure of the
Temple School. Fourth child, Abba May, born in Concord.
1842. ABA Travels to England. Meets Thomas Carlyle and Charles Lane.
**1844. ABA moves with his family to Harvard, Massachu-
setts, where he and Charles Lane found the Fruitlands
commune.**
**1845. Fruitlands fails. The Alcott family, destitute, moves to
Still River.**
1857. ABA returns with family to Concord after living in Boson and Wal-
pole, New Hampshire. Goes on lecture tours.
1858. Daughter Elizabeth dies in Concord.
1859. ABA appointed superintendent of schools in Concord.
1872. *Concord Days* is published.
1879. ABA opens Concord Summer School of Philosophy.
1888. Dies in Boston on March 4.

At Fruitlands, Amos Bronson Alcott founded a commune where he hoped to live a perfect life. He believed that, given the right place and the right conditions, adults could recapture child-like innocence. Fruitlands, he hoped, would be that place. Before he got there, he and Charles Lane, a principal member of this new family, planned a daily routine which would perfect spiritual life by purifying the body: a regimen of cold baths, celibacy, vegetarianism, and temperance.

He had no money to invest in Fruitlands, but Charles Lane put up $2000. Lane and Samuel May, Alcott's brother-in-law, who had helped support the Alcotts for years, bought a run-down farm in Harvard, Massachusetts.

The Alcotts and friends arrived on June 1, 1843. They had traveled in the rain from Concord, their possessions, including a large bust of Socrates, crammed into a wagon. Amos Bronson Alcott's wife, Abba, sat in front with their baby, Abigail; Louisa May Alcott rode in the back with her sister Beth. Bronson went on horseback, and Anna, the eldest, walked the fifteen miles, splashing through puddles.

The early-eighteenth-century farmhouse, the dilapidated barn, and the fallow meadowland all needed attention. There were three rooms on the first floor: two front rooms and a long, narrow, back kitchen running the width of the house. Bronson and Lane chose the right front room for their library of about a thousand volumes, the most important and valuable possession of the group, and soon hired a carpenter to build a hundred feet of shelving.

The left front room became Bronson's study. He and Abba took the bedroom above it, on the second floor. Lane slept in the bedroom over the library, and his son slept in the small connecting hall between the two bedrooms. Visitors and other members of the commune, which had eleven members at its largest, bedded down on straw in the large room over the kitchen. The four Alcott children slept in the attic under the low eaves, their beds against the large chimney in the center of the house.

At Fruitlands, the children were free of some of the pressure of parental disapproval, since they saw the adults around them behaving in such odd ways. One free-speech advocate believed that words themselves had no power to harm, it was the way you said them. Each morning, he greeted people with a cheerful, "Good morning, damn you." Another man, who believed all emotions should be freely expressed, shouted from the tree tops when he was happy and lay on the floor and moaned and wept when he was sad. The children, who had been lectured to all their lives, went mad with delight at these antics. For their sakes, Bronson Alcott made sure that Samuel Bower, a nudist, confined his naked experiments to night rambles in the woods, after the children were asleep.

Once Lane and Alcott settled on a routine, they had the children—Anna, 12; Louisa, 10; and Elizabeth, 8—get up at five to take cold, outdoor showers, before a singing lesson with Lane. After breakfast, they washed dishes and did their chores: cleaning, sweeping, and dusting. There was usually time to play, before studies began at 10 am. After writing, spelling, and arithmetic lessons, Lane sometimes read the children a story with an obvious moral.

Bronson and Lane expected the children to take part in philosophical discussions. On a day when there was more work than play, the ten-year-old Louisa May Alcott wrote in her diary: "Anna and I did the work. In the evening, Mr. Lane asked us, 'What is Man?' These were our answers: A human being; an animal with a mind; a creature; a body; a soul and a mind. After a long talk we went to bed very tired."

The diet at Fruitlands was bland and unstimulating: no alcohol, coffee, tea, cocoa, milk, cheese, butter, pork, beef, mutton, fish, salt, or spice of any kind. For breakfast they ate porridge, unleavened whole-wheat bread made from unrefined flour, and water; for lunch more bread, vegetables, and water; the same for dinner, except fruit instead of a vegetable.

In a time of unhealthy dietary practices in the industrial nations, particulary among the growing urban poor, the members of the Fruitlands commune were searching for a cleaner, healthier way of life, but their perfectionism not only led to impractical extremes, it also required hard work. The men talked, while the women did the work.

At one point, Alcott and Lane decided that members of the commune would wear brown linen costumes: the men, a tunic over full pants; and the women, a tunic over a full skirt. Silk and cotton were forbidden because, they believed, silk manufacture exploited worms, and cotton, the slaves who picked it. The heavy, coarse, brown linen costumes were difficult to farm in, and even more difficult to launder. Abba, who did all the washing, scrubbed the clothes on a wooden scrub board.

During the late summer, just before the harvest, Alcott and Lane took off for New York City in their brown linen costumes on a roving philosophers' tour. They planned to give talks about spiritual progress and communal life at Fruitlands. After each talk, they asked for donations. Unadvertised and unknown, they depended on reform organizations to host them. The audiences were small and Bronson came home with empty pockets. Just before he returned, Abba and the children harvested as much of the barley crop as they could.

Abraham Everett, one of the members of the commune, was the only man who helped with the housework. Mostly, the hard work was done by Abba and her children: hauling water from the well, sewing, cleaning, cooking, and baking at the woodstove for the eleven commune members and their frequent guests.

Bronson's plan for perfection made Abba's life more difficult. He and Lane outlawed whale oil for lamps and bought bayberry wax for candles, but discovered that they didn't know how to make them. The men were willing to go to bed at night, but Abba, whose solitude came after the children were asleep, rebelliously lit her oil lamp.

By fall, people began leaving for various reasons, the work was too hard, the food poor, Bronson Alcott tyranical and impractical. Anne Page, who was supposed to help Abba with the housework, was hounded out because she had eaten fish at a neighbor's house.

As the weather turned colder, it became clear that the meager harvest of barley and rye from unfertilized fields— Bronson and Lane refused to use unclean manure—would not get the community through the winter. They had not planted root crops like parsnips, carrots, and potatoes, which could be stored over the winter, because, they thought, fruits and vegetables which grew underground were degraded. Even though fruit was a staple in their diet, there were only ten apple trees at Fruitlands.

Worn out and afraid, Abba told Bronson she had to leave and would take the children with her. She felt she had lost her husband. For months, the couple argued about sex. Influenced by Lane, Alcott stopped making love. He told Abba that sex was physically weakening, spiritually debasing, and separated them from the rest of the group. She and Bronson were the only couple among a community of abstinent men.

The children felt their parent's unhappiness. On her mother's birthday, October 8, 1843, Louisa wrote in her diary, "I wish I was rich, I was good, and we were all a happy family this day."

Before Christmas, Alcott threatened to leave his family. He felt that he couldn't be a philosopher and support a wife and four children at the same time. Louisa was frightened, she wrote in her diary, "Anna and I cried in bed, and prayed to God to keep us all together." Alcott left for Boston to join Lane, and Abba and the children spent Christmas alone at Fruitlands. When he returned, he withdrew from his family, stopped eating, and sank into a depression. His dream for a paradise in Harvard, Massachusetts was over.

The Alcotts moved to Still River in mid-January 1845. The commune had lasted less than a year. After the break-up of Fruitlands, Abba supported the family by working as a domestic, as a city missionary to the poor in Boston, and, later, as the manager of a domestic employment agency.

The Fruitlands Museums were founded by Clara Endicott Sears, and the red farmhouse which she restored was opened to the public in 1914.

The Old Manse
Concord, Massachusetts

Nathaniel Hawthorne

Nathaniel Hawthorne

Monument Street
Concord, Massachusetts 01742
617-369-3909

Open April 17-May 31: 10 am-4:30 pm, Saturdays; 1 pm-4:30 pm, Sundays
and Holidays. June 1-October 31: 10 am-4:30 pm, Monday, Thursday, Friday, Saturday; 1 pm-4:30 pm, Sundays and Holidays. Admission—Adults,
$2.50; Children 12-16, $1.00; Children under 12, $.75. Parking in lot across
from house. Restrooms on edge of parking lot. Also of interest as home of
Ralph Waldo Emerson. Adjacent to North Bridge battleground, site of the
first forcible resistance of the Revolutionary War. Flower garden. Open
field and wooded area from house to the bank of the Concord River.

1804. Born July 4, Salem, Massachusetts to Elizabeth Clarke Manning
Hawthorne and Nathaniel Hawthorne.
1808. NH's father dies in Dutch Guiana.
1825. NH graduates from Bowdoin College and returns to mother's house
in Salem where he lives for twelve years.
1828. NH pays for the publication of his first novel, *Fanshawe*.
1837. *Twice-Told Tales* published.
1839. NH is engaged to Sophia Peabody. Works as a measurer in the Boston Custom House.
1841. NH joins the Utopian community of Brook Farm, withdrawing
before the end of the year.
**1842. NH marries Sophia Peabody on July 9 and moves to the
Old Manse in Concord, Massachusetts.**
1844. Una, the Hawthorne's first child, born in Concord.
**1846. NH moves to Salem and becomes Surveyor of the Port.
Mother dies and his son, Julian, is born.**
1850. NH becomes well-known with the publication of *The Scarlet Letter*.
1852. The Hawthornes move to The Wayside in Concord. *The Blithedale
Romance* published.
1853. NH appointed United States Consul at Liverpool by his friend,
President Franklin Pierce.
1858. The Hawthornes live in Italy.
1860. The family returns to America and The Wayside. *The Marble Faun*
is published.
1864. Dies on May 18, in Plymouth, New Hampshire.

Nathaniel Hawthorne and Sophia Peabody were married in Boston on July 9, 1842 and spent their wedding night at The Old Manse. Their honeymoon in Concord, Massachusetts lasted three years. From the first days, they were ingeniously surprised to discover the pleasure of sex. They were also stunned to find that ordinary daily intimacy—meals, walks, reading together—could make them so happy.

Physical joy had not seemed possible for either of them. Before he married, Hawthorne had lived a deeply solitary writer's life. After graduating from Bowdoin, he refused to enter a conventional profession that would give him a secure income. Instead, he returned to his mother's house in Salem, Massachusetts. An introvert herself, his mother respected his need for privacy and gave him the time and place to write.

However, as he turned thirty, knowledge of life drawn only from books seemed cold and lifeless. On a visit to the Peabody family in Salem, he met Sophia Peabody. They had much in common. Both felt shadowy, unreal, cut off from affection and vital life. Sophia, who, like Hawthorne, was born in Salem, had lived as a recluse since she was nine. Sensitive, prone to excruciating headaches, she was dosed with drugs and encouraged in her invalidism as if it would be her life's work. She told Hawthorne that she had lived in a seclusion as deep as his own.

Their marriage brought the Hawthornes into vivid immediate contact with the physical world. They felt alive, newly created by love. The world was real. They could feel it. They called themselves the new Adam and Eve. Everything they wrote during their stay at the Old Manse—in letters and diaries—conveys the pleasure of well-matched lovers who luckily, and against all odds, find sex delightful from the beginning. Sophia rejoiced that she was completely his. Her headaches stopped.

The abyssmal condition of their new house couldn't depress their high spirits. The Old Manse was the family home of the Emerson's, built in 1770 by the Reverend and Mrs. William Emerson, whose son, William, was the father of Ralph Waldo Emerson. Before the Hawthornes, the house was occupied by Reverend Ezra Ripley, Mrs. Emerson's second husband and Ralph Waldo Emerson's stepfather. Reverend Ripley survived his wife and lived on at the Old Manse. Increasingly feeble in his final years, he couldn't make the stairs and slept in the downstairs front parlor. When the Hawthornes moved in, in 1842, they found everything coated with years of accumulated dirt—the walls, ceilings and woodwork were, according to Hawthorne, "a dismal tinge of brown," the furniture "rheumatic" except for a highboy rearing "an absolute tower of mahogany to the ceiling."

Hawthorne immediately moved the grim portraits of seventeenth- and eighteenth-century ministers out of his study. He and Sophia painted and decorated, brightening the gloom with silver candlesticks, lamps, and bronze and alabaster flower vases, which they filled daily with white lilies, brilliant-red cardinal flowers, and violet pickerelweed. Through the airy spacious front hall, they could look straight through the house to the back meadows and the river. The upstairs hall was large enough to be a room in its own right.

There was more space than they needed. On the first floor, there were two front parlors on either side of the hall and, at the back, a kitchen and a small dining room. The back upstairs chamber over the dining room became Hawthorne's study. He and Sophia slept in the room over the right front parlor. Across the hall, was another front bedroom, which they used for guests. Hawthorne preferred open fires. However, for comfort and economy he put in three wood-burning stoves, one in the large slope-floored kitchen.

The Hawthornes stayed close to home. They loved the weathered clapboards, overgrown in places with clumps of moss, which seemed to add to the seclusion of the gambrel-roofed house. Hawthorne wrote that "the figures of passing strangers looked too remote and dim to disturb the sense of privacy." In The Old Manse, they felt the presence of previous lives, the many couples they now joined in the real events of life: marriage, birth, and death.

Their days fell into a simple order. They rose early. Hawthorne bathed in the river or worked in the garden, breakfasted with Sophia at nine, and spent the rest of the morning in his upstairs study, while Sophia painted in the dining room directly below. When she finished a painting, she etched a record on the studio window. Her words are still there: "Endymion painted in this room—finished January 20, 1844." After a mid-day dinner, their principal meal, they walked, rested, ate a light supper, and spent the evenings reading.

The butcher came two or three times a week, the milkman everyday. Hawthorne planted a vegetable garden next to the long path to the front door. Living, as he says, with "as much easy trust in Providence, as Adam," his only anxiety consisted of "watching the prosperity of [his] vegetables." Their ripeness matched his contentment; he describes the gold winter squash, "turning their great yellow rotundities to the noontide sun."

There was also a large orchard of apple, peach, pear, and cherry trees, as well as quince and current bushes, planted by Reverend Ripley during his retirement. For the first time in his adult life, Hawthorne was in tune with the natural world. He wrote, "In the stillest afternoons, if I listened, the thump of a great apple was audible, falling without a breath of wind from the mere necessity of perfect ripeness." He had matured as a lover, as a husband—accepted, touched, tasted, and found delightful.

Pleasures he could taste and smell became more important than writing, but he still spent a good part of the morning in his small second-floor study. The two back windows, shaded by a willow, which swept against the eaves, looked out to the orchard and the river. On the side wall, a third window overlooked the battleground. So he wouldn't be distracted by the view, Hawthorne built a folding desk against the windowless wall next to the fireplace. No larger than the seat of a dining-room chair, it held just paper and an ink-pot.

His Concord friendships were consistent with his Concord pleasures: he was drawn to Thoreau, who sold him a boat and taught him how to row. Hawthorne described Thoreau's mastery, "Mr. Thoreau managed the boat so perfectly...that it seemed instinct with his own will, and to require no physical effort." Hawthorne couldn't row as well, but he was soon triumphantly taking the boat out alone, fishing at dawn, and bringing back a dozen bream for the cook to fry up for breakfast and dinner.

Although warned that she was too weak for normal married life, Sophia quickly recovered from a miscarriage in her first year at the Old Manse — "Man's accidents are GODS Purposes" she scratched on the window of the upstairs study. The next year Sophia went through a normal pregnancy. Hawthorne helped with the housework, laying the fires in the kitchen and bed-room, making tea and light meals when the cook was away. On Thanksgiving, with Sophia healthy and six months pregnant, they happily feasted alone on pudding, turkey, custards, and pies.

On March 3, 1844, Sophia gave birth to her first child in the upstairs bedroom at the Old Manse. They named the baby Una. Hawthorne began to think more about money. He had earned a little from his writing — rent was low, $100 a year — and he expected to recover the investment he had made in the Brook Farm commune, where he had lived for a short time before his marriage. But when that money was lost, he had to look for work.

In 1846, Samuel Ripley, the Reverend Ezra Ripley's son, notified Hawthorne that he wanted to move into the family home. While the Hawthornes were still there, workmen began preparing for the Ripley's return, repairing outbuildings, and, to Hawthorne's disgust, scraping away the old mosses from the clapboards.

From Concord the Hawthornes moved to Salem, where Hawthorne was appointed surveyor of the port. There he arranged the tales for *Mosses from the Old Manse*, some of which he wrote in Concord, adding a preface with material from the journal had kept during his long and happy honeymoon.

The Old Manse, Hawthorne's name for the Emerson-Ripley home, remained in the Emerson family until 1939, when it was acquired by The Trustees of Reservations, restored, and opened to the public.

The Wayside
Concord, Massachusetts

Nathaniel Hawthorne

Nathaniel Hawthorne

455 Lexington Road (Route 2A)
Concord, Massachusetts 01742
617-369-6975

Open April 1-November 1, 9:30 am-5:30 pm, Thursday through Monday.
Last tour at 5:00 pm. Admission—Senior Citizens (with Golden Age Pass),
no charge; Adults, $.75; Children 15-under, no charge. Parking directly
across the street. View of Concord from Nathaniel Hawthorne's unusual
tower-study. One of the settings for Louisa May Alcott's *Little Women*. Of
interest as the home of the Alcotts, Hawthornes, and Margaret Sidney,
author of *The Five Little Peppers and How They Grew*.

1804. Born July 4, Salem, Massachusetts to Elizabeth Clarke Manning
Hawthorne and Nathaniel Hawthorne.

1808. NH's father dies in Dutch Guiana.

1825. NH graduates from Bowdoin College and returns to mother's house
in Salem where he lives for twelve years.

1828. NH pays for the publication of his first novel, *Fanshawe*.

1837. *Twice-Told Tales* published.

1839. NH is engaged to Sophia Peabody. Works as a measurer in the
Boston Custom House.

1841. NH joins the Utopian community of Brook Farm, withdrawing
before the end of the year.

1842. NH marries Sophia Peabody on July 9 and moves to the Old Manse
in Concord, Massachusetts.

1844. Una, the Hawthorne's first child, born in Concord.

1846. NH moves to Salem and becomes Surveyor of the Port. Mother dies
and son, Julian, is born.

1850. NH becomes well-known with the publication of *The Scarlet Letter*.

**1852. The Hawthornes move to The Wayside in Concord. *The
Blithedale Romance* published.**

**1853. NH appointed United States Consul at Liverpool by his
friend, President Franklin Pierce.**

1858. The Hawthornes live in Italy.

**1860. The family returns to America and The Wayside. *The
Marble Faun* is published.**

1864. Dies on May 18, in Plymouth, New Hampshire.

The Hawthornes moved at least seven times in the first ten years of their marriage. By 1850, after the publication of *The Scarlet Letter*, Hawthorne's novels were earning money and critical praise, and he looked forward to settling down in his own home.

In 1852, Hawthorne bought the Alcott's Hillside house for $1,500, immediately changing the name to The Wayside, because it stood so close to the road that it could have been mistaken for a coach stop. The Alcotts had lived there from 1845 to 1848 and had renovated the original, early-eighteenth-century, four-room colonial farmhouse. On the west side, Bronson Alcott had added a two-story wing: a study and two small rooms on the first floor, and two rooms on the second. On the east side, he had built a bathhouse and woodhouse.

Pleased to have paid so little for the enlarged house, Hawthorne was sure he would eventually be comfortable, once he and Sophia cleaned it up. Although the house was crammed between the road and a steep hill which rose sharply from the back wall, the front, south-facing rooms were filled with sunlight most of the day. The study Alcott had built was far enough away from the busy common rooms of the house to give Hawthorne the privacy he needed.

Sophia arrived with her daughters, Una and Rose, a few days before her husband and set to work. Her enthusiasm for a new carpet, an astonishing shade of rich lapis lazuli, carried her along as she arranged furniture and hung pictures. After all her many moves, Sophia enjoyed decorating her own house. For the first time in her married life, she felt she was coming home to stay.

Shortly after Hawthorne arrived at The Wayside, Franklin Pierce, a college friend from Bowdoin who was running for President, asked Hawthorne to write a campaign biography. Hawthorne was ambivalent about the request. He didn't like being indebted to Pierce, and he became uneasy about his own ambition. He believed that the biography would insure Pierce's favor, but would not enrich his own creative life. He was at a critical point. Pierce's request came just after he had finished *The Blithedale Romance*. He was between books, waiting for an idea to shape itself. Though he still felt ambivalent, he agreed to write the biography.

Once he had made his decision, he worked quickly. On July

28, 1852, shortly after he began writing, his sister Louisa died when the steamboat on which she was a passenger burned and sank. Despite the loss, he finished the Pierce biography on August 27.

He then turned to children's stories, a form he loved. His retelling of classical myths was published as *Tanglewood Tales*. However, planning a novel had become impossible. In November, Pierce was elected President, and Hawthorne was immediately besieged by office-seeking friends and relations whom he tried to help, including Herman Melville, who came to Concord hoping to find a political appointment.

President Pierce offered Hawthorne the Consulship to Liverpool. Attracted by the salary, the honor, and the chance to travel, Hawthorne accepted and immediately made preparations to leave The Wayside. Breaking with his past life, he burned boxes of old papers and letters. Among them were hundreds of letters from a friend or lover whose name he kept secret:"What a trustful guardian of secret matters is fire! What should we do without fire and death?"

On July 6, 1853, as the *Niagra* sailed out of Boston Harbor, Nathaniel Hawthorne, the new Consul to Liverpool, was saluted with a cannonade. He would publish only one more novel, *The Marble Faun.*

The Wayside was empty most of the time the Hawthornes were away. However, when Horace Mann, the husband of Sophia's sister, Mary, died in the summer of 1859, Sophia invited Mary to move to The Wayside with her three sons. They stayed until the Hawthornes' return.

The Hawthornes arrived back in Concord in 1860, after seven years abroad and, immediately began renovations on The Wayside. Soon, all but Hawthorne felt at home. Sophia quickly involved herself and her children in Concord life. She taught Sunday school in the new front room she called the Chapel. She was regularly "at home" every Wednesday afternoon, and she and the children frequently visited the Alcotts who now lived in Orchard House, the next house to The Wayside on Lexington Road. When Louisa May Alcott returned from the Civil War, ill with typhoid, Sophia invited May, the youngest Alcott daughter, to eat all her meals at The Wayside.

Sophia enjoyed decorating and entertaining. For a large

coming-out party for Una, she filled The Wayside with the best roses she could find from the Emersons' garden and the garden of her horticulturalist neighbor, Ephraim Bull. She loved transforming the rooms and opening the doors to a festive scene: the table laid, the carpets and furniture moved away, the floors bare for dancing.

During the party, Hawthorne descended from his private study to visit with guests. Although he was intimate and loving with his family, to others he remained a distant figure. Bronson Alcott said that Hawthorne behaved like a "foreigner...his moats wide and deep, his drawbridges...up on all sides... Nobody gets a chance to speak with him unless by accident."

There were many reasons for his remoteness. His fame set off awestruck reactions which he could not stand, but more disturbing was his worry about Una. For almost the entire year before returning to America, he had been worn down by her serious illness, a particularly severe case of "Roman fever," or malaria, which almost killed her. Una's emotional swings had frightened him for years. In his journal, he described her as "a spirit strangely mingled with good and evil, haunting the house where I dwell." Hawthorne called his final year in Europe the worst of his life. Soon after returning to Concord, Una became ill again, and Hawthorne believed it was a recurrence of malaria, until it became clear that Una was having a mental breakdown. She was violent and had to be restrained. Although she responded to treatment, she was unstable for the rest of her life.

In addition to Hawthorne's worries about Una, he was afraid that his long stay abroad had made it impossible for him to feel at home in Concord. In Europe, he was happy to be away from political controversy. In Concord, every thinking person talked politics and causes. Hawthorne bolted when he saw visitors coming. He would hurry out the back door and up to the crest of the hill behind the house, where the path he wore by his restless pacing could be seen long after his death. His distaste for Concord's liberal and abolitionist fervor made him an outsider. Although he eventually sided with the North because he despised the Fugitive Slave Law, he found the abolitionists destructive and called John Brown, a hero to all Concord liberals, a "blood-stained fanatic" who was "justly hanged." The Hawthornes, unlike their neighbors, the Emersons and Alcotts, refused to send their daughters to a coeducational school. Sophia believed that studying with members of the opposite sex would be far too stimulating for already overheated adolescents.

If Hawthorne had been pleased with his new renovations, he might have been more comfortable at home. His workmen had built a second-floor bedroom above what had originally been Hawthorne's study and changed the study into a library. Above this bedroom, Hawthorne built a third-floor tower study based on his memory of a Florentine villa.

The renovations were a disaster. Because of its disproportionately high ceiling, the new bedroom looked like a deep narrow box. Although the tower-study had a wonderful view, the elevation was so steep as to make the long flight of stairs almost unmanageable. The room was hot in summer, freezing in winter, yet a woodstove made the room too stifling to work in. Hawthorne hated the results and wrote that he had "transformed a simple and small old farmhouse into the absurdist anomaly... if it would only burn down."He used his study in the spring and fall, and then hardly at all.

Hawthorne was having trouble writing fiction, and after *The Marble Faun* in 1860, he did not complete another novel. He returned to travel pieces, which gave him income and relieved him of trying to force his imagination. The first-floor library and the tower room were the scenes of a persistent labor of will which did not flower into art. He left four unfinished novels.

He began complaining of unusual fatigue. He may have already been affected by the illness—most likely cancer—which in 1862 began to weaken him even more, until he could not climb the stairs to his study.

In May of 1864, Hawthorne, knowing he was dying, started on a carriage ride to New Hampshire with Franklin Pierce. They rented rooms at an inn in Plymouth. That night Hawthorne died in his sleep.

After his death, Sophia and Una left The Wayside to live in England, where both eventually died and were buried. From 1881 until 1882, Julian Hawthorne's wife and their six children lived in the Wayside. Hawthorne's daughter, Rose, sold the house in 1883 to Daniel Lothrop, whose wife was Margaret

Sidney, the author of *The Five Little Peppers and How They Grew*. After Margaret Sidney's death in 1924, her daughter inherited The Wayside, opening the house to the public in 1927.

Orchard House
Concord, Massachusetts

Louisa May Alcott

Louisa May Alcott

399 Lexington Road (Route 2A)
Concord, Massachusetts 01742
617-369-4118

Open April 1-September 15, 10 am-4:30 pm, Monday through Saturday,
1 pm-4:30 pm, Sunday; September 15-October 31, 1 pm-4:30 pm, everyday.
Restoration in process: call ahead to double-check times of opening.
Admission—Senior Citizens, $1.75; Adults, $2.50; Children 6-17, $1.25;
Children under 6, no charge. Parking in lot directly in front of Orchard
House. Ask to see wildflower garden and the Hillside Chapel, which
housed Bronson Alcott's School of Philosophy. Call or write ahead for
schedule of poetry readings, plays, talks, and special children's events.

1832. Born November 29 in Germantown, Pennsylvania to Abigail May
    Alcott and Amos Bronson Alcott.
1837. LMA attends the Temple School run by her father in Boston.
1840. LMA lives with her family in Edmund Hosmer's cottage in Concord
    and becomes a student of Thoreau's at Concord Academy.
1843. With her family, LMA becomes a member of Utopian community,
    Fruitlands, in Harvard, Massachusetts.
1845. LMA moves from Still River, where Alcotts lived after Fruitlands, to
    Hillside House (renamed The Wayside by Hawthorne) in Concord, one
    of the settings of *Little Women*.
1850. LMA works as a domestic in Needham. Returns to Boston to teach.
1854. LMA has first story published in a popular magazine under pseudo-
    nym; publishes her first book, *Flower Fables*, under her own name.
**1858. Her sister Elizabeth dies. LMA moves into Orchard
    House in Concord with her family.**
1860. Writes first novel, *Moods*, published in 1864.
**1862. LMA leaves in December to serve as an army nurse in
    Washington, D.C.**
**1863. Back in Concord on January 23, LMA is seriously ill
    with typhoid. *Hospital Sketches* published.**
1868. LMA writes first volume of *Little Women*.
1869. Second volume of *Little Women* published.
1870. LMA takes tour of Europe.
1877. Mother dies.
1888. Dies in Roxbury on March 6, without knowing her father had died
    two days before.

In 1858, with $500 from Ralph Waldo Emerson and $450 donated by other friends, Louisa May Alcott's father, Amos Bronson Alcott, bought Orchard House in Concord, Massachusetts, a ten-acre property which included two buildings, an early seventeeth-century farmhouse and a tenant house.

Bronson Alcott planned and supervised the joining of the farmhouse and tenant building and took charge of the subsequent renovations and additions. After the changes, the family had a spacious, airy house. On the left of the front center hall was Bronson Alcott's large book-lined study and, to the rear of the study, was a north-facing studio with skylights for May, the youngest Alcott daughter and the artist of the family. To the right of the hall was the bright south-facing front parlor, which opened onto a dining room.

Louisa May Alcott was uncertain and drifting, and she never developed an attachment to Orchard House. In Concord, she chaffed against the restraints of a daughter's life. Five-foot-eight, tall for a woman of her time, enormously energetic and strong, Alcott neither looked nor acted like her graceful and demure sisters. In her teens, she realized she was unusual, and wrote, "I...don't care much for girls' things. People think I'm wild and queer; but Mother understands and helps me." She dreamed of being a great writer, a great actress, and a heroic nurse. But at the age of twenty-six, when she moved into Orchard House, she had only a string of dreary jobs to her credit and only one published story. In Boston, where she tried to find work in the fall of 1858, she felt lonely and hopeless. Poor, depressed, alone, and unable to find work, she walked around Boston and thought of suicide. She looked down over the edge of the Mill Dam into the Charles River, but stopped herself from jumping in. It would be cowardly, she said, to give up.

After this low point, her life began to change. She was offered and took a one-year position as a governess in Boston for $250 a year, and was able to support herself, send money home to Concord, and help May, who came to Boston for art lessons. In the fall of 1859, the *Atlantic Monthly* accepted one of her stories. When it was published in March, her father, proud and pleased, rode to the village and bought a copy of the magazine for her. With confidence from this small but definite success, Alcott went on with her writing.

Her sister Anna was married in May 1860, in the front parlor of Orchard House. Alcott wrote in her diary that the house was "full of sunshine, flowers, friends and happiness." Alcott had twined lilies of the valley in her sister's hair and had watched family and friends dance around the bridal pair on the lawn under the Revolutionary elm, but she sought a different kind of success. Louisa May Alcott never married. Her mother's marital unhappiness because of her father's refusal to support the family had turned Alcott against marriage. She wanted a man who respected her genius. Thoreau, whom she loved, was not interested in women.

Three months after her sister's wedding, Alcott began and finished her first novel, *Moods*. Working day and night in her room at Orchard House, she had a first draft in four weeks. The *Atlantic Monthly* bought another story for $50, and in January, 1861, she revised *Moods*, working even harder on the second draft. She closed herself in her room and hardly slept or ate. She released herself into her work.

After her success at the *Atlantic Monthly*, Alcott looked ahead, "I've not been pegging away all these years in vain, and may yet have books and publishers and a fortune of my own." However, for a short time, her writing career did not progress. The editor of the *Atlantic*, even though he bought her stories, steered her to teaching. She needed the money. She wrote in her diary, "Don't like to teach, but take what comes; so when Mr. F. offered $40 to fit up with, twelve pupils, and his patronage, I began." Even when the kindergarten was unsuccessful, her former editor told her, "Stick to your teaching. You can't write." She told him, "I won't teach, and I can write; and I'll prove it."

She returned to Concord and continued to write serious stories, and what she called "lurid" stories for the well-paying, illustrated newspapers. But she was still restless and dreamed of heroic escapes. The Civil War gave her an opportunity. In December 1862, a month after her thirtieth birthday, Alcott began nursing at the Union Hotel Hospital in Washington, D.C.

The work was heavy, the hospital foul, and conditions unhealthy. In January, she contracted typhoid and was given large doses of calomel, a drug which contained mercury. Her father went to Washington to bring her home. They arrived in

Boston on January 22, and the next day took the 4 pm train to
Concord. Nathaniel Hawthorne's daughter, Una, a friend of
the Alcott sisters, was on that train and held Alcott in her
arms. Una's mother wrote to a friend that Alcott was "like a
sheaf of flames."

Her old room at Orchard House became a sickroom. Delir-
ious from high fever, she had nightmarish visions and could
not be left alone. Her family nursed her, day and night, her
father taking the night watch. They all believed she would die.
Their next-door neighbors, the Hawthornes, tried to help and
invited May to take meals with them.

In February, the fever began to subside, and on February 22,
Alcott came downstairs for the first time. On March 22, her
father wrote in his journal, "Louisa leaves her chamber and
begins to clothe herself with flesh after the long waste of
fever." The fever was gone, but she was left with the effects of
mercury poisoning from the calomel. Painful sores covered her
mouth. She was bald. Her hair, once thick, grew back thin and
scanty. For the rest of her life she suffered from severe pains,
chills, weakness, and restlessness.

As she had done in the past, Alcott turned to work. In the
spring, in her room at Orchard House, she edited the letters
she had written to her family from Washington. They became
the popular *Hospital Sketches*, which made her reputation and
created an audience for the earlier *Moods*, which was finally
published in 1865.

Editors were now eager for her work and pressed her with
their suggestions, trying to make her into a popular writer.
They didn't want unusual adult novels like *Moods*. Thomas
Niles, a publisher, urged her to write a girls' book. Back in her
room at Orchard House, after working in Boston as an editor of
a children's magazine, she began *Little Women*. Throughout
May, June, and part of July 1868, she wrote every day at the
small lap-sized desk between the front south-facing windows,
her books and favorite pictures on the mantel to her right. By
July 15, she had finished the first volume, which was published in September and sold well. She started the second
volume in November in a furnished room in the South End of
Boston and finished it in January 1869.

By August 1871, 82,000 copies of *Little Women* had been
sold, and 42,000 of *Little Men*. Success intensified Alcott's

need to provide for her family. Writing children's books, which she called, "moral pap," did not draw on her exuberant genius as *Moods* had. But, now she saw herself as a great provider, not a great writer. When her right hand became crippled from illness and years of writing, she trained herself to write with her left hand so she could still turn out at least a book every year, long after there was any need for money. Though circumstance had left her the job of spinster-drudge, a private role that was too small for her, she tried to make it a destiny that approached greatness.

She had always given money to her parents and sisters. With the $600 she earned from *Hospital Sketches*, she payed for May's Boston art course, had Orchard House reshingled, and bought firewood, coal, food, and clothes. After the publication of *Little Women*, she paid off the family's long-accumulated debts. In 1871, Alcott had a furnace installed, so that Orchard House would at last be warm. She was deeply satisfied that her mother would finally have a peaceful, care-free life.

Alcott hardly ever stopped working. She needed to be needed. When her sister Anna's husband died, she began *Little Men* in order to earn more money to support her sister, even though Anna's husband, John Pratt, had left Anna and her two sons well-provided for. In 1877, Alcott bought the old Thoreau house on Main Street in Concord for Anna.

As for her own life, she moved back and forth between Orchard House and various rented apartments and houses in Boston. Even with all the improvements she had made to Orchard House, she never enjoyed Concord. For so long, she had been caretaker, housekeeper, and money-maker for her parents. In 1873, Bronson wrote: "Under Louisa's supervision our housekeeping for the last fortnight has sped quietly and tidily. And it is gratifying to find that she has lost nothing of her practical cunning while engaged in writing stories for the million." But Alcott was not superhuman. When obligations at Orchard House overwhelmed her, she took off for Boston.

Nevertheless, caring for her family became her reason for living and working. When her mother died in 1877, she could hardly go on. When her sister May died two years later in Europe from complications following childbirth, Alcott, according to May's wishes, took charge of her sister's child, Lulu. Lulu came to Concord in 1880, and gave her aunt a new focus for concern and generosity. Alcott, who had always worn hand-me-downs when she was growing up, had beautiful dresses made for her niece, everyday dresses and red-velvet party dresses trimmed with white lace.

Alcott's painful spells brought on by the mercury poisoning became more severe. After her father's stroke in 1883, she finally decided to sell Orchard House and moved her whole family into a house on Boston's Louisburg Square. Later, her father lived with Anna in Concord. In 1887, Louisa May Alcott moved into a Roxbury nursing home, where she died on March 6, 1888, two days after her father's death. She was fifty-six. She had published 270 poems, novels, and stories. Her fortune went to her surviving family.

William Torrey Harris, who later became the United States Commissioner of Education, bought Orchard House in 1884 and later sold it to Harriet Lothrop, who wrote popular children's books under the name of Margaret Sidney. In 1911, the Concord Woman's Club bought the house and began raising money for its restoration. It was opened to the public in 1911.

The Ralph Waldo Emerson House

Concord, Massachusetts

Ralph Waldo Emerson

Ralph Waldo Emerson

Cambridge Turnpike at Lexington Road
Concord, Massachusetts 01742
617-369-2236

Open April 15-October 31, 10 am-4:30 pm, Friday through Saturday;
2 pm-4:30 pm, Sunday. Admission—Adults, $2.50; Children 6-17, $1.00;
Under 6, no charge. Parking directly in front. Be sure to see exceptional
flower and vegetable garden. Additional books, furniture, memorabilia
from Emerson's home on display at the Concord Antiquarian Museum,
directly across the street.

1803. Born May 25, Boston, Massachusetts to Ruth Haskins Emerson and
    William Emerson.
1811. William Emerson dies.
1821. RWE graduates from Harvard.
1829. On March 11, RWE is ordained as pastor of Second Church, Boston;
    on September 30, RWE marries Ellen Tucker.
1831. Ellen dies of tuberculosis on February 8.
1832. RWE resigns as pastor and travels to Europe.
**1835. RWE marries Lydia (Lidian) Jackson. They move to
    Concord where RWE lives for next forty-seven years.**
**1836. RWE's Brother Charles dies; his first book, *Nature*, is
    published; and his first child, Waldo, is born.**
1841. Publication of the first volume of *Essays*.
1842. RWE's son, Waldo, dies of scarlet fever on January 27.
**1855. RWE receives copy of *Leaves of Grass* and writes to
    Whitman, "I greet you at the beginning of a great
    career."**
**1862. RWE lectures in Washington, D.C. and talks with Pres-
    ident Lincoln.**
**1872. Concord house is damaged by fire. RWE travels to
    Europe.**
**1882. Dies on April 27. Buried in Sleepy Hollow Cemetery,
    Concord, Massachusetts.**

Ralph Waldo Emerson was free-thinking, but conventional in his daily life. A friend to eccentrics, rebels, and reformers, Emerson, nevertheless, lived a middle-class life of regularity, responsibility, and order. The closest Emerson came to making his household more democratic was when he uneasily invited the servants to join the family at meals. He was relieved when they refused.

His wife, Lidian, ridiculed reformers, especially those who lectured on the nutritional and moral value of eating unleavened bread. Her no-nonsense views and solidly middle-class tastes expressed a side of Emerson he did not always reveal to his radical friends.

Theirs was not a marriage of passion. Emerson had adored his first wife, Ellen Tucker, and she, by openly and freely expressing her love in an unreserved way, had drawn Emerson out of his lonely solitude. After her death from tuberculosis, he was sure he would never love with all his heart again.

In 1834, Emerson and Lidian Jackson planned for a responsible married life in their future home in Concord, which he bought before their wedding for $3,500. They invited Emerson's mother, Ruth, and his younger brother, Charles, who was also soon to be married, to live with them. Before they moved in, Emerson added a back parlor on the northwest corner, which, with the bedroom above it, would provide an apartment for Charles and his future bride, Elizabeth Hoar.

After Emerson and Lidian were married, Emerson took possession of his new house and looked forward to a happy life. He had finally recovered from his first wife's slow, painful death, and was delighted to learn that there had never been a death or funeral in his new home.

After the Emersons moved to Concord in 1835, Charles and Elizabeth were forced to postpone their marriage when Charles contracted tuberculosis. In 1836, Charles died, never having lived in his brother's new home.

Built by the Coolidge family, the house was only six years old when the Emersons moved in. The location, directly on Lexington Road and a half mile from the town center, lacked privacy, but the house was spacious: four-over-four large, airy, high-ceilinged, corner rooms, with windows on two sides. On the south side of the house was an ell, which housed the kitchen and rooms for the cook and housemaid.

In addition, there was a large barn/shed with a hayloft. To the southeast, Emerson planted extensive flower and vegetable gardens as well as raspberries and blackberries. Lidian brought her favorite old-fashioned roses and Holland bulbs from her former home in Plymouth, New Hampshire.

She also contributed the Jackson family furniture. Emerson's mother brought Emerson family furniture and her maid. Ruth Emerson lived with her son for almost twenty years. When she became too feeble to use the stairs, she took the large front room on the first floor, directly across from her son's study.

She and Lidian never fought. Although their relationship could, at times, be tense, it was always controlled. No matter what unspoken differences she had with her daughter-in-law, Ruth Emerson found life, in Concord, reassuringly predictable and secure.

The family rose early. The servants were called to the dining room for morning prayers, which were followed by breakfast. After breakfast, Emerson would take his daily walk to the post office, stopping at the butcher and the grocer to place the daily orders, which would be promptly delivered to the kitchen door before the midday meal. After his mile-long walk, Emerson returned to work in his study. Dinner, the principal meal of the day, was served at one o'clock. Unlike his temperate vegetarian friends, Emerson loved a hardy meal which included meat and, occasionally, wine. After dinner, the Emersons wrote letters, hurrying to finish them in time for the afternoon mail to Boston.

Order and regularity served Emerson's genius. He finished writing *Nature*, his first book, in a comfortable rocking chair, placing his manuscript on a large atlas which spanned the arms of the chair. From the two front windows of his study, he could easily see Lexington Road and, when the windows were open in warm weather, could hear the shouts of the children in the schoolyard directly across the road. He did all his writing here: essays, poetry, lectures, journal entries, and letters.

In this high-ceiling room with a black marble fireplace and a somber painting of the three Fates, he received his friends and, as his fame increased, the many callers who came to Concord. He became a public man, even in his own home.

Directly across the hall from Emerson's study is the room

where all the Emerson children were born. Lidian had four children in nine years. The first was Waldo, who died of scarlet fever at the age of five; and the last, Edward, who was born when Lidian was forty-one. She was deeply attached to her children, who grew up counting on the unvarying regularity of the household.

If there were conflicts in the Emerson house, they were never directly expressed. Emerson would send a crying child from the table to look at the clouds. Edward, the youngest, remembered that he was never able to resist his father's gentle control. A calm order prevailed.

Emerson acknowledged his coldness and reserve. On the lecture platform, he drew people to his public persona, but when his wife and friends sought real affection, he could not open up.

He was a benefactor to Thoreau and Alcott, a role which eventually created distance between him and them. Yet, both Thoreau and Alcott were sometimes able to draw Emerson out of himself.

Thoreau lived with the Emersons in 1841, taking the small, second-floor room at the top of the stairs, now a bathroom. In exchange for room and board, Thoreau tended the garden and made himself useful as an all-around handyman. Later, Thoreau built his cabin on Emerson's land at Walden Pond and returned from Walden to live again as caretaker in Emerson's house when Emerson traveled to Europe on a lecture tour.

Emerson lectured more and more as his family grew. He was a popular speaker, attracting an audience eager for secular alternatives to religion. The press accused him of being an atheist. Emerson had given up his ministry in the Unitarian Church, yet he was the minister of the Transcendental Movement, testifying to the worth of personal revelation.

Between 1833 and 1881, he gave almost fifteen hundred lectures in twenty-two states and Canada—eighty-three towns—not counting his European tour. Travel gave him an outlet for his restlessness—particularly his extended tour in Europe from October, 1847 through July, 1848.

Writing home from abroad, he addressed each of his letters to the entire family. Lidian, longing for a personal letter, felt neglected. While he was away, she read the letters Ellen Tucker had sent to Emerson, and longed for her husband to write her the kind of letters that, so long ago, had inspired Ellen's loving response. Emerson could only acknowledge his failure to love Lidian as she wanted to be loved—passionately.

On July 24, 1872, he and Lidian were home alone, except for the servants. They were awakened by the crackling sound of fire behind their bedroom wall. Emerson ran out into the pouring rain in his nightgown, shouting for help. Neighbors came, then firemen. Most of the books, furniture, and papers were saved. The roof was destroyed, but the walls stood. Rain poured into the smoke-blackened rooms. The Emersons believed that the fire started when a maid overturned a kerosene lamp in the attic.

Emerson and Lidian temporarily moved to The Old Manse. Emerson became ill; he was demoralized and uprooted. He missed his peaceful study, which had contained the work of his lifetime. All his papers, journals, letters, and manuscripts had been dumped into boxes.

Friends raised money to send Emerson to Europe and to rebuild the house. His first daughter, Ellen Tucker Emerson, named for Emerson's first wife, went with him.

When they returned, a great crowd turned up at the train station in Concord to welcome Emerson back. A brass band played "Home Sweet Home." Emerson walked under an arch of flowers into his rebuilt home, his treasured books and papers back in their familiar places in his study.

In the following years, he wrote less and less. His memory failed, and he relied more and more on his daughter Ellen. Never marrying, she took care of her parents until her father's death in 1882 and her mother's death in 1892.

Ellen Tucker Emerson lived in the family home until her own death in 1909. The house is still owned by the Emerson family, who have opened it to the public.

Walden Pond

Concord, Massachusetts

Henry David Thoreau

Henry David Thoreau
Photo courtesy of Concord Free Public Library.

Walden Pond State Reservation
Route 126 (near junction of Route 2)
Concord, Massachusetts 01742
617-369-3254

Open daily, 8:30 am-dusk (no later than 8 pm). Supervised swimming June
1 through Labor Day, 10 am-7 pm. Boats *without motors* allowed. Parking
lots on Route 126, across from pond. $3.00 per car during the summer.
Self-guided walks to site of Thoreau's house. Guided tours, "Thoreau
Ramble," mid-June to the end of August, 10 am and 3 pm, Monday
through Friday; 10 am, 1 pm, 3 pm, Saturday and Sunday; tours begin at
the Contact Station in the main parking lot. Call for information about
special programs.

1817. Born July 12 in Concord, Massachusetts to Cynthia Dunbar
   Thoreau and John Thoreau.
1837. On August 30, HDT graduates from Harvard. Teaches at Concord's
   Center School but resigns rather than administer corporal
   punishment. Begins his journal.
1839. HDT becomes director of Concord Academy.
1840. HDT proposes to Ellen Sewell. She accepts, but is forced by her
   family to break engagement because the Thoreaus are shockingly
   liberal.
1841. HDT moves to Emerson's house in Concord, where he works for the
   Emersons in exchange for his room and board.
1842. HDT is traumatized by the death of his brother, John.
1843. Tutors Emerson's three nephews in Staten Island.
**1845. In the Spring, HDT plants two-and-a-half acres of
   vegetables in a field near Walden. He builds a house on
   the shore of Walden Pond and moves in on July 4.**
**1846. On July 32, HDT is arrested and imprisoned overnight
   for refusing to pay poll tax.**
**1847. HDT leaves the house at Walden on September 26 with
   the manuscripts of his first two books, *A Week on the
   Concord and Merrimack Rivers*, and *Walden*, both written
   during his stay. Moves to the Emerson house in the fall
   for a year's stay.**
1848. In July, HDT advertises his services as a surveyor and begins work.
1849. May 14, "Civil Disobedience" is published. *A Week on the Concord
   and Merrimack Rivers* is published on May 30.
1854. *Walden* is published on August 9.
1859. HDT's father dies on February 3, and HDT takes over the family
   pencil-making business. On October 30, HDT speaks in defense of
   John Brown.
1862. After having been ill with tuberculosis for more than five years,
   HDT dies on May 6.

Before moving to Walden Pond, Thoreau supported himself by teaching and by working as an all-around handyman for the Emersons in Concord, Massachusetts. Like other members of the Transcendental Club he met through Ralph Waldo Emerson, Thoreau wanted to find a way to survive without being enslaved to a job. At the age of twenty-eight, he decided to simplify, reduce his possessions, and live off the land. At the end of March, 1845, he began building a one-room, ten-by-fifteen-foot house on a woodlot belonging to Ralph Waldo Emerson above the shore of Walden Pond. By the fall of 1845, he had dug the cellar, laid the floor boards, and raised the walls and roof. The king-post was an entire tree which went from cellar to ridge-pole, the highest horizontal timber in the roof. In November, as the weather turned colder, Thoreau built the chimney from second-hand bricks and stones from the shore, where he also found white sand for his mortar. Next he plastered the walls to keep out the December cold.

The completed house, with a separate wood shed in the back, was, according to Thoreau, "tight and light." One room served as kitchen, bedroom, parlor, and storeroom, and contained the essentials, among them: a lamp, a spoon, a cup, an oil jug, and a jug for molasses. He was not interested in complication or beautiful decoration: beauty was best appreciated outdoors, where it didn't have to be dusted or polished.

He wrote that he did not want to die without knowing the real nature of life. He wanted, "to live deep and suck out all the marrow of life, to live so sturdily and Spartan-like as to put to rout all that was not life." If life were evil, he wanted to face that evil; if life were divine, he wanted to know that divinity through his own experience.

In the two years and two months he spent at Walden, from July 4, 1845 to September 6, 1847, Henry David Thoreau found the exhilarating self-reliance he searched for. Supporting himself through occasional odd jobs and by selling the beans he grew near the cabin, he had plenty of time to write, explore, and think.

At Walden, Thoreau completed *A Week on the Concord and Merrimack Rivers*, and the first draft of *Walden*. With compass, chain, and sounding line, he disproved the legend (which still persists) that Walden is a bottomless pond. A 1939 sounding of the pond's deepest point is only two-tenths of a meter greater than Thoreau's figure of 102 feet.

At the end of his first summer at the pond, strengthened by the initial success of his experiment in self-reliance, Thoreau found an action consistent with his abolitionist beliefs. He refused to pay taxes to a government which supported slavery. For this, he was arrested and spent a night in the Concord jail.

Thoreau's passion for narrow simplicity took him into smaller places than his one-room cabin. He believed that houses were merely porches over the entrances to animal burrows in the earth. He had dug the cellar of the cabin in the side of a hill, taking note that a woodchuck had burrowed there before him. He even described his head—brain and imagination—"as an organ for burrowing." He used his mind "as some creatures use their snout and forepaws." With it, Thoreau said, he would burrow his way through the hills which surrounded Walden. The earth was his true home, the cabin only a flimsy porch. As he watched foxes in winter, he felt they were "rudimental, burrowing men...awaiting their transformation."

Sometimes roaming through the woods like a starving beast, wanting to rip the throat of a deer, Thoreau understood his kinship with the flesh-eaters. However, Thoreau found animal food unclean and did not eat fresh meat.

He also found civilization unclean. Life in the animal burrow at Walden was fresh because it was solitary and uncrowded. He believed that people crowded together in huge city buildings were like vermin. He wrote that real connections only occurred between people when they were far enough from each other for "all animal heat and moisture" to evaporate. He loved animals in nature, but the animal in man was sensual and reptilian.

In his cabin, he sought to live a chaste, solitary, and abstemious life, restricting himself for the sake of economy and purity, to a diet without milk, butter, coffee, tea, and fresh meat. For bread, he mixed rye and cornmeal and baked the small loaves on an open fire.

Simplifying life, he tested his endurance and experienced the exhilaration of survival. But he was not completely solitary and self-sufficient: almost daily he walked to Concord to see his family; his mother did his laundry. But he needed few other people beside his family.

The earth was his lover. He discovered at Walden that it was like the human body, "covered with papillae" and as sensitive as human flesh. Into the earth he went, mining old stumps with axe and shovel, as if they were deep veins of gold.

Thoreau sat in the open doorway of his house from dawn till noon, deep in meditation. The earth and the sky were the connected poles of his existence. He found what he called "heaven's own blue" in the pond, in the snow, in the eye of the bird. The bird's eye seemed to him to have been created with the sky. These reflections were his eternity. In winter, he deliberately made holes in the snow to see the way they reflected the blue sky.

At Walden, Thoreau lived the life he had imagined for himself. He was not disappointed. Rather than evil, he found wildness. He believed that without wildness, life would stagnate. When life at the cabin had become routine, he left Walden Pond and moved back to Concord.

Later, Emerson's gardener, Hugh Whelan, moved the house farther from the pond, intending to enlarge it. He got as far as digging the foundation for the new wing, but it was never completed. After a time, Thoreau's house slid into the foundation hole. In 1849, what was left of the cabin was hauled by ox team to the Clark farm north of Concord and used as a storage shed, and, later, pulled down. Eventually, the salvaged lumber was used to patch the Clark barn.

There is no house on the shore of Walden Pond today. Granite markers outline the site of Thoreau's one-room house above the north cove.

Craigie House
Cambridge, Massachusetts

Henry Wadsworth Longfellow

Henry Wadsworth Longfellow

105 Brattle Street
Cambridge, Massachusetts 02138
617-876-4491

Open 10 am-4:30 pm, Daily. Admission—Senior Citizens, no charge;
Adults, $.50; Children under 16, no charge. On-street parking. Restrooms
in back of house. Headquarters of George Washington. Original Longfellow furniture, books, paintings. Box-bordered garden designed by Longfellow. Longfellow park across the street. Call ahead for information on
special events. Tours of Tory mansions on Brattle Street are held in fall.

1807. Born February 7, in Portland, Maine to Zilpah Wadsworth and
Stephen Longfellow.
1825. HWL graduates from Bowdoin College.
1826. HWL travels to Europe for a three-year study trip.
1829. Bowdoin names HWL Professor of Modern Languages.
1831. On September 14, HWL marries Mary Storer Potter of Portland,
Maine.
**1836. Mary Potter Longfellow dies in Europe where HWL had
gone to study. HWL becomes Professor of Modern
Languages at Harvard.**
**1839. *Voices of the Night* and *Hyperion*, HWL's first two books,
are published.**
1843. On July 13, HWL marries Frances Appleton.
1844. Charles, the first of six children, is born, June 9.
1847. *Evangeline* published.
1854. HWL resigns from Harvard.
1855. *The Song of Hiawatha* is published.
**1861. Fanny Appleton Longfellow dies in fire in Craigie
House.**
1882. Dies March 24.

Henry Wadsworth Longfellow first met Fanny Appleton in Switzerland in 1836. She was only nineteen. He immediately fell in love with her, even though he was still mourning his recently dead wife.

A few years later, Longfellow, now a professor at Harvard and settled in his rented rooms at Craigie House in Cambridge, Massachusetts, began to call on Fanny at her father's home in Boston. Fanny Appleton was lively, beautiful, accomplished, and rich. She called Longfellow "the professor." He read dull German ballads to her. She found him stuffy, and discouraged his attentions.

He kept coming back, boring her with his pedantic recitations, until he finally had the courage to tell her that he loved her. Longfellow asked her to marry him, and after taking time to decide, Fanny sent a note to him, accepting his offer. As soon as he read the note, he walked from Craigie House, in Cambridge, to her father's house on Beacon Street, in Boston.

At the time of their engagement, Longfellow was renting two second-floor rooms at Craigie House. Although it needed redecorating, Craigie House was structurally sound. Fanny and her father saw advantages in owning the house. Longfellow could easily walk to work at Harvard, and Cambridge, at that time a small village, was a quiet, healthy place to bring up children. The house looked out on the Charles River and its traffic of sailboats and schooners. Fanny's father gave them Craigie House for a wedding present. To insure their view of the river, Fanny shrewdly asked her father to buy up the land across the street.

The Tory mansion had been built in 1759 by Royalist Major John Vassall. He abandoned Craigie House when the Revolutionary forces approached Boston in September 1774. General George Washington appropriated the house in July 1775. His wife, Martha, joined him in December, and they stayed on together until March 1776. The house made an impressive military headquarters, with its eleven-foot-high ceilings and elaborate wainscotting and carved woodwork. There were four large rooms on the first floor, four large rooms on the second floor, and five smaller rooms in the attic.

Andrew Craigie, the first Apothecary General of the American Army, bought the house in 1791. He added two side piazzas and a two-story back ell, which contained a kitchen and additional rooms above. The old kitchen, at the left-rear of the center hall, became the dining room. Craigie decorated the former kitchen with a black-marble mantel, wainscotting, and carved woodwork. He enlarged the library at the right-rear of the house, making it into a huge twenty- by thirty-foot ballroom with its own entrance, so guests arriving by carriage could enter the ballroom directly.

When the newly-married Longfellows moved in, Henry Wadsworth Longfellow was not enthusiastic about taking care of a large, old house. He was, however, interested in the grounds. He directed the gardener, one of five servants, to plant an avenue of Lindens on the north border and planted a small, romantic, lyre-shaped garden. Later, he expanded this lyre shape into a box-bordered Gothic garden, whose formality contrasted with the great hedges of old lilac and original apple trees.

Fanny took charge of the interior. She wrote that she was comfortable in the library "with its cozy *fauteuils* [armchairs], and goodly bookcases, topped by plaster worthies, its tiled fireplace, [and] old-fashioned mirrors," but she turned the parlor into a ladies drawing room with a "modern aspect," wallpaper, drapes, and carpet all covered with bright red and pink roses. Fanny wrote to her brother, describing her evenings at home, "Fancy Henry playing a nocturne while I lounge by the fire in a comfortable *fauteuil* and you have our afterdinner look to life."

The Longfellows liked modern comfort. Craigie House was among the first houses in America to have indoor plumbing. They installed central heating in 1850 and gaslight in 1853. At first, the brightness of gaslight shocked Longfellow. Every room looked like a lit-up ballroom. Previously, except for holidays and parties, lamps and candles had been used sparingly.

Longfellow had learned the art of hospitality in Europe. An attentive host, he knew how to listen to his guests and avoid controversial subjects. He found politics too violent for dinner-table conversation. He talked about poetry.

He loved a party with beautiful women in colorful dresses, champagne and music, and lamps hung in the trees. He arranged the wines and fruits and flowers and selected ruby-red Bohemian goblets decorated with gold grape-vines for the wine. In the early years of their marriage, he and Fanny led a very social life. He invited his friends home for whist and for billiards in the special billiard house he built in the garden. He and Fanny gave musical evenings in the library and dinner parties where they liked to serve game: venison, canvasback ducks, grouse, and pheasant from England. They went to every important opera, concert, and play and heard every important speaker who came through Boston. Craigie House became a stop for the famous, singer Jenny Lind, actress Fanny Kemble, Charles Dickens, William Makepeace Thackery, and the Polish patriot, Kossuth.

Longfellow spent quieter times at home with old friends. His closest friend was the abolitionist Charles Sumner, who in 1856 was nearly beaten to death on the floor of the Senate for his anti-slavery views. Sumner, before he went to Washington to serve in the U.S. Senate, spent every Sunday at Craigie House. Longfellow kept his friends for life and enshrined their likenesses. For his study, he had Eastman Johnson, a well-known artist, do a group of oval, charcoal portraits of Sumner, Ralph Waldo Emerson, Nathaniel Hawthorne, and Cornelius Felton, a fellow professor who would later become President of Harvard.

Longfellow wrote with the portraits of his friends around him. His study, at the front of the house, across from the parlor, and to the immediate right of the front door, had been George Washington's office. Longfellow decorated it with dark-red drapes, a flowering lemon tree, a round table in the center of the room, a standing desk near the front window, and a deep, leather armchair in front of the coal fireplace, all of which was reflected in a convex, girandole mirror above the fireplace. Longfellow either wrote at the center table, at the desk, or, when his eyes were bothering him, in the armchair, in front of the fire, writing in pencil without looking at the page.

For years, Longfellow wanted to leave Harvard, so that he could spend more time on his writing. In 1854, he finally resigned and, almost immediately, began *Hiawatha*, which was published in the fall of 1855. It was an enormous popular success, by January, selling 300 copies a day. Actors read it in theatres to full houses.

Longfellow continued in his orderly daily routine, producing one success after another. In 1840, he had been paid $15 a poem; by 1874, $3000.

Longfellow carried fame lightly, but sometimes wondered how he could be father of a family, uncle of America, and helper of the dispossessed foreigners who came through Boston. He hardly ever refused the beggars who came to the porch.

The Longfellows could afford to give their children anything they wanted. For birthdays there were magic lantern shows; *tableaux vivant*, with the children dressing in costumes; and supper and dancing in the parlor. At Christmas, Fanny would write each child an affectionate, encouraging letter from Santa Claus. Year round, she kept a record of their sayings in the "Chronicle of Craigie Castle."

The Longfellow's first child, Charles, was born in 1844, and the sixth, Anne Allegra, in 1855. After having trouble nursing Charles, Fanny was delighted to be able to breastfeed her second child.

Frances, their third child, died of fever at two, and the Longfellows were terrified whenever another child got sick, but their remaining children thrived, surviving illnesses and accidents. Charles, who, unlike his father, loved loud noises, rough play, and guns, accidently shot off his thumb with the gun his parents finally allowed him to buy with his savings.

The Longfellows were very attached to one another. Only once in their marriage were they separated, when Longfellow spent two days on a pleasure trip in New Hampshire in 1860. Fanny called Anne Allegra their "love child", and signed one of her rare letters to Longfellow, "A long, long kiss just here." They still used the small, simple, country sleigh-bed they had slept in on their wedding-night.

On July 9, 1861, Fanny was sealing packets of the children's locks of hair for keepsakes. Her gauzy dress caught fire. She ran to her husband, who threw a rug around her, and tried to beat out the flames with his hands. Her face, which she pressed against his chest, was unburned. She died the next day. Longfellow thought he was going to go mad.

Fanny's funeral was held in the library. Longfellow was too badly burned to attend. Flowers covered the coffin; a wreath of orange blossoms circled Fanny's head. She looked younger than her forty-four years.

Loneliness followed horror and shock. Very slowly, Longfellow returned to a regular life.

His friends helped him through these years. But eventually, he outlived most of them. Felton died in 1862, Hawthorne in 1864, and Sumner in 1874. Longfellow lived long enough to see the birth of two grandchildren. Edith's son, Richard Henry Dana III, was born in the southwest bedroom of Craigie House in 1879.

Longfellow died in Craigie House in 1882, and was buried next to Fanny in the beautifully landscaped groves of fashionable Mt. Auburn Cemetery.

Craigie House remained in the Longfellow family until 1973, when it became a National Historic Site, maintained by the National Park Service.

The John Greenleaf Whittier Home

Amesbury, Massachusetts

John Greenleaf Whittier

John Greenleaf Whittier
Photo courtesy of Haverhill Public Library.

86 Friend Street
Amesbury, Massachusetts 01913
617-388-1337

Open May 1-October 31, 12 noon-5 pm, Tuesday through Saturday; winter
by special appointment, call ahead. Admission—Adults, $1.00; Children
under 12, $.50. On-street parking. As home of Quaker abolitionist and
poet: religious, historical, and literary interest. Collection of papers,
books, and memorabilia. Fine examples of women's domestic arts of the
nineteenth century made by Whittiers and their friends. Remarkable
saucer magnolia in bloom in early May; flower garden at its best in July.

1807. Born December 17, Haverhill, Massachusetts to Abigail Hussey
   Whittier and John Whittier.
1826. Editor William Lloyd Garrison publishes JGW's poem in the
   Newburyport *Free Press*.
1827. At twenty, JGW enters Haverhill Academy; leaves in 1828.
1830. Father dies. JGW becomes editor of *New England Weekly Review* in
   Hartford.
1831. JGW's first book published.
1835. JGW is elected Representative to Massachusetts Legislature.
   Attacked by anti-abolitionist mob in Concord, New Hampshire.
**1836. JGW moves to Amesbury, Massachusetts with mother,
   sister, and aunt.**
**1840. JGW returns to Amesbury after resigning from
   Pennsylvania Freeman.**
1843. *Lays of My Home* is published.
1855. Mother dies.
**1859. JGW breaks off near-engagement with Elizabeth Lloyd
   Howell.**
1864. Sister Elizabeth dies.
1866. "Snow-bound" is published.
1892. Dies September 7, in Hampton Falls, New Hampshire.

After his father's death in 1830, John Greenleaf Whittier stayed on at the family farm in Haverhill, Massachusetts with his unmarried brother and sister, Elizabeth, his mother, Abigail, and his Aunt Mercy. When his brother married and moved away, Whittier was unable to manage the farm alone. In 1836, the Whittiers sold the homestead, where their family had lived for five generations. Whittier and his mother bought a small, salt-box cottage on Friend Street in Amesbury, just across from the Friends' meeting house, for $1,200.

At first they were miserably homesick for the large farm and felt shut up in the five-room cottage in Amesbuy. There was not much space: two tiny bedrooms, a kitchen, a small parlor; and an attic room. After they moved in, in 1836, they added a small bedroom on the southeast side for Aunt Mercy.

They no longer had to make the twenty-four mile trip to Quaker meeting, which was the focus of Abigail Whittier's week. She was serious and spiritual. The life of the mind was more important to her than the life of the body. She was a devout Quaker and passed on her habits and beliefs to her son. They celebrated no holidays, including Christmas. They distained luxury and valued frugality, cleanliness, and simplicity.

Abigail Whittier was an excellent manager, and she religiously clung to old-fashioned ways. She kept house with habitual meticulous care. Her linen was spotless. She wasted nothing and spent little. She and her daughter still made their own clothes and wove some of their own linen. They did not put in a kitchen stove; instead, they cooked in a large open fireplace, which took up almost one wall of the kitchen. The heavy iron pots hung directly over the flame. They baked all of their bread, pies, and cake in a brick-lined wall-oven, heated by its own fire-box.

Skilled farmers, they were able to live out of their half-acre garden: storing apples, carrots, onions, turnips, and squash over the winter, and preserving grapes, peaches, and quinces from their vines and fruit trees.

By the time the Whittiers moved into their Amesbury home, John Greenleaf Whittier had built a reputation as a journalist and abolitionist. He left Amesbury, to become the editor of the *Pennsylvania Freeman* in Philadelphia. After a few years, his health broke down, and, in 1840, suffering from insomnia, blinding headaches, and chest pains, he returned to

Amesbury, to the protective care of his mother. This was not the first time that leaving home had brought on such agonizing symptoms. His bond to his mother was the strongest attachment in his life. Whittier belonged to his mother.

He had always admired men of action, and, for a while, he had managed to live an active life. He had worked as a lobbyist for the Anti-Slavery Society, a job that required some travel; he had risked his life against an anti-abolitionist mob in New Hampshire and had, in Philadelphia, disguised himself and gone into the destroyed offices of his newspaper in Pennsylvania Hall, after it had been burned by a mob of twenty thousand, to rescue whatever records he could find.

But from 1840 on, he drew what he believed were safe boundaries around his life, avoiding situations and emotions which would bring on episodes of excruciating pain. Whenever he felt a strong emotion, he would experience a suffocating pressure in his chest, head, and throat. His doctor told him to avoid travel. He obeyed. In returning to the safety of his mother-ruled house, he gave up a measure of freedom for a measure of health and the security to write.

Between periods of ill health, he was a great worker. From the cottage in Amesbury, he edited two Massachusetts newspapers, and as corresponding editor contributed 275 articles and 109 original poems to the abolitionist *National Era*. He went on with his political work, helping to elect liberal candidates to the United States Senate, and opposing in print every government action which might promote slavery.

The gifts of Joseph Sturge, a wealthy Quaker benefactor, supplemented Whittier's small income. Between 1841 and 1848, Sturge gave Whittier $3,000. With part of this endowment, Whittier enlarged the cottage, adding a plain kitchen at the back of the house. He built a second-story dormer on the east side and also expanded his aunt's old bedroom, which, after her death in 1846, had become Whittier's study. Over this study, which he called the Garden Room, Whittier added a second-story bedroom for his sister.

The Garden Room, now heated by an elegant wood-burning parlor stove, became the center of his working life. Since the publication of *Lays of My Home* in 1842, his reputation as a poet had grown. James Fields, Whittier's editor, realizing that Whittier was a tremendous worker whose poetry might have a large public appeal, skillfully managed his career, and, in 1857, Fields obtained all the copyrights of Whittier's previously published poems. By the 1860s, Whittier was selling poems to the well-paying *Atlantic Monthly* and royalties were accumulating on the dozen books of poetry Fields had published. In 1866, *Snow-Bound* made Whittier famous, earning $10,000, the most he had ever made on a book.

He had written *Snow-Bound,* as well as most of the poems of his middle and late period, in the Garden Room of the cottage. A poor sleeper, he wrote mostly at night. Although he easily wrote prose in clear, elegant, flowing script, which needed few revisions, he worked hard on his poems. The first drafts were disorganized and illegible. Final copies came after labored revisions. In his later years, he worked with a local printer who ran off galleys, so Whittier could revise more efficiently.

Despite the fame *Snow-Bound* brought, Whittier did not believe he was a great poet whose work would survive. Self-criticism, study, care, and laborious rewriting had produced works which touched a wide public, but he was scrupulously honest about what he felt were his shortcomings. He recognized that he wasn't a master poet, no matter what his worshipful public believed.

The success of *Snow-Bound* nevertheless made his life easier. Editors, who formerly refused to publish him because of his radical views, now welcomed his work. To a public in need of virtuous father figures who were neither ministers nor priests, Whittier became a national hero. He had risked his life against pro-slavery mobs, worked for more than thirty years to abolish slavery, and in his poetry combined the moral conscience of the North with a nostalgia for the simplicity of rural life. He now became a moral star.

His public invaded his privacy. He was moved by the poised, well-dressed, black Jubilee Singers of Fisk University, who sang for him in the parlor of the Amesbury House, the women in silk dresses looking so different from their slave mothers and grandmothers. He was also hounded by sight-seers, interviewers, autograph-seekers, and people asking for money, endorsements, and poems for special occasions and causes. He could not walk on the street without being stopped. His house had become a station on the "pilgrim's" route. He complained of 150 ministers dropping in, of cranks who traveled around the world and made Amesbury their last stop. They came in all weather, unannounced, with requests and praise. Whittier's seventieth and eightieth birthdays were public events. For the latter, the Governor of Massachusetts and other dignitaries traveled by special train to Danvers, where Whittier was staying with cousins. He had become a hero to a public who needed to worship aged patriarchs.

He took this mass adulation with wry modesty. But, it was no substitute for real friendship. Nevertheless, his literary life had brought him many friends. Ralph Waldo Emerson, Oliver Wendell Holmes, and James Russell Lowell all visited Whittier in Amesbury. They sat in the Garden Room, which had its own entrance facing Friend Street. Whittier made a ritual of tending the fire. In late April and early May, the white and pink blossoming magnolia filled the two back windows. He hung the walls of his personal sanctuary with pictures of his friends who were especially important to him.

When young he had been in love with a distant cousin who rejected him. Later, he felt that his lack of money and the responsibility for his mother and sister held him back. The closest Whittier ever came to marriage was to Elizabeth Howell in 1859, four years after the death of his mother. But no woman was able to replace his mother or his sister, Elizabeth.

As he grew older, Whittier felt he had missed something good by not marrying. He outlived the women he loved. His Aunt Mercy died in 1846, his mother in 1855, and his sister in 1864.

After his sister's death, Whittier's brother's daughter, Elizabeth, kept house for her uncle. She married in 1876, and Whittier began spending his winters with cousins in Danvers, returning to Amesbury for the summer.

The house on Friend Street became a memorial to his mother and sister. When he opened the house each spring and stepped into the parlor, he saw their portraits facing each other on opposite walls—his mother's serious, sad face dominating the room. There were other reminders of Abigail Whittier, a memorial wreath of fading, dried flowers encircling her photograph. He thought of his mother and sister when he looked ahead to his own death: "I have the instinct of immortality, but the conditions of that life are unknown. I cannot conceive what my own identity and that of dear ones gone before me will be."

His last visit to Amesbury was in May 1892, when he, as he had done for many years, held open house for the Quarterly Meeting of the Society of Friends.

He died on September 7, 1892 in Hampton Falls, New Hampshire, nine miles from Amesbury, and his body was laid out in the small portrait-hung parlor of the Friend Street house. Hundreds of mourners packed together in the back garden overflowing the seats that had been set out in rows. He was buried in the Union Cemetery in Amesbury in Quaker fashion, with no ceremony.

In 1918, the Whittier Home Association bought the house which had been occupied by Whittier's niece.

New Hampshire

The Frost Farm
Derry, New Hampshire

Robert Frost

Robert Frost

Route 28 and By-pass 28
Derry, New Hampshire 03038
603-432-3091 (July and August)
603-271-3556 (The Division of Parks and Recreation)

Open Memorial Day-last week in June, 9 am-5 pm, weekends only; Last
week in June-Labor Day, 9 am-5 pm, Wednesday through Sunday. Times
of opening subject to change, call ahead. Admission—Senior Citizens
(New Hampshire residents only), no charge; Adults, $2.00; Children under
18, no charge. Free parking in the lot on the north side of the house.
Guided tour, two films, a tape of Frost reading his poetry, and an exhibit
of photographs interpreting Frost's work. Take the self-guided, half-mile,
poetry/natural history trail.

1874. Born in San Francisco, California on March 26 to Isabella Moody
    Frost and William Prescott Frost, Jr.
1885. RF's father dies, moves with his mother and sister to New
    Hampshire.
1895. RF marries Elinor Miriam White, a classmate at Lawrence High
    School in Lawrence, Massachusetts.
1896. RF's son, Elliott, born.
1899. Daughter Lesley is born. RF withdraws from Harvard after two
    years.
**1900. First child, Elliott, dies of cholera. Frosts move to
    Derry, New Hampshire in October.**
1906. RF begins teaching at Pinkerton Academy in Derry.
**1909. Frost family leaves Derry farm and moves to Derry
    Village.**
1913. RF goes to England with family. His first two books are published in
    England.
1923. RF wins Pulitzer Prize for *New Hampshire*.
1930. Daughter Marjorie dies of puerperal fever.
1938. Elinor Frost dies.
1940. Carol, his only surviving son, commits suicide.
1942. RF wins his fourth Pulitzer Prize for *The Witness Tree*.
1961. RF reads "The Gift Outright" at John F. Kennedy's inauguration.
1963. Dies in Boston on January 29.

Depressed and ill at the age of twenty-six, Robert Frost thought he was going to die of tuberculosis. His wife, Elinor, went to his grandfather to ask for help. William Frost agreed to buy his grandson a farm and sent a relative to Derry, New Hampshire to inspect a property.

The simple, white, Greek Revival farmhouse, built in 1884, needed only a coat of paint. The rooms were plain and small-ish, but sufficient: a side hall on the left and three rooms lined up on the right: a bay-windowed front parlor, a dining room, and a kitchen. The sitting room opened to a south-facing porch on the right, and a small north room on the left, which could be used as a sewing room or an extra bedroom. There were three bedrooms upstairs, the largest over the front parlor. Out back, a door from the kitchen led to the connecting woodshed and barn.

Across Londonderry Turnpike, opposite the house, were two small pastures; to the east of the house, a hay field and a woodlot; to the north, a vegetable garden; to the southeast, a carefully pruned, well-tended apple orchard. The owner had also planted peach, pear, and quince trees.

Satisfied with a positive report, William Frost bought the thirty-acre farm for $1,700, plus $25 for a few tons of hay left in the barn. He held the deed and gave use of the farm to the Frosts.

William Frost made arrangements for the care of the farm. He hired Carl Burell, an old friend of Robert Frost's who knew farming, to live with the Frosts and help out. William Frost gave Burell money to buy a cow and a horse and wagon. Burell would care for the cow, the horse, the fruit trees, and the garden; whatever profit he made on the sale of the surplus would be his. Frost would run the hen business.

In October 1900, Frost moved to the farm with his wife, Elinor, and their daughter, Lesley. He was exhausted by the move and resented his grandfather's taking charge. His poor health and depression got worse after his mother's death in November 1900. She had always supported him and soothed his night fears: he slept in her room until he was eighteen. Feeding the chickens, taking in the eggs, hauling in water from the outdoor pump, the kitchen floor so cold that spilled water froze, he alternated between anger and self-loathing. He thought of suicide.

He was still grieving from the death of his son, Elliott, who had died of cholera three months before the move to Derry. He held himself responsible and believed that his delay in calling a doctor caused the child's death. He had never finished college, leaving both Dartmouth and Harvard without getting a degree, and he doubted that he could earn enough money from the hen business to support the family. He knew that his wife was disgusted with his inability to make a living. Since their courtship days, she had recoiled from sex, and her continuing fastidiousness made Robert feel like a bestial ravisher. To his other failures, he added his failure as a lover and a husband.

Eventually, life on the Derry Farm got better for the Frosts. He and Elinor found that they shared a passionate love for wildflowers and the change of seasons. By spring, Robert Frost's grief subsided and he regained his health. Although he hated the hen business, he found something of his own at Derry: the farm became the seed-bed for his poems. He took hold of life and flourished.

He worked a little—to get by, and to have time to write. As he went through the poems he'd been writing since high school, choosing the strongest and making new drafts, he began to think of himself as a poet again. In the evenings, after the others had gone to bed, he would sit up late at the kitchen table near the woodstove, writing many of the poems that would eventually go into his first three books, *A Boy's Will* (1913), *North of Boston* (1914), and *Mountain Interval* (1916). He went on working in obscurity; between 1894 and 1906, he sold only five poems.

Nevertheless, he continued to put himself into his writing, and into wildflowers, and into family life. About his writing he was sometimes doubtful, but he was never doubtful about his passion for flowers. He found early orchis, bluets, adder's tongue, lady's slipper, jack-in-the-pulpit, yellow violets, and a white-flowered hobble-bush, and transplanted them to the banks of Hyla Brook, in a place the Frosts called "the park." In midsummer, he would wade up to his knees in the cranberry bog to pick pogonias: rose-pink, iridescent, wild orchids.

He taught his four children to love flowers. Three were born at the farm: his son, Carol, in 1902; daughters Irma and Marjorie, in 1903 and 1905. As they grew, they joined their parents in walks along Hyla Brook. The seasons were their great events: the first hot sun in March, the first flower, the first bluebird, the first falling leaves, the first snow. They picked chestnuts in the fall, tender dandelion shoots in spring, and wildflowers in succession.

Robert and Elinor Frost led their children into nature. They learned botany in the woods and in their park. In the journal that she began when she was five, Lesley Frost names forty-seven flowers and shrubs, among them five varieties of wild orchid. Frost set up a telescope in an upstairs window and interested his children in astronomy by presenting each with a star to follow.

Except for occasional visits from relatives, the family enjoyed their simple pleasures alone: birthdays with cake, banana pudding, and candy; at Halloween, four jack-o'-lanterns shining in the dark house; at Christmas, a spruce tree in the front parlor decorated with candles; for July 4, a small-town celebration in the village. In 1909, the Frosts had their first Thanksgiving turkey and decided that chicken was better.

Frost and his wife had grown closer; they shared the farm, the care of the children, the clear sound of Hyla Brook at night when they went out to get water, and the wild orchids which they both loved. However, Elinor still felt bitter that she had sacrificed her own aspirations for her husband and children. And Frost was insanely jealous of his wife's intellectual gifts.

Sometimes the violent undercurrents of the Frost's marriage came out in fierce arguments. Lesley remembered her father once waking her in the middle of the night and bringing her down to the kitchen where Elinor was seated at the table. Frost held a loaded revolver and told Lesley to choose between him and Elinor because one of them would die. Elinor quieted the child and took her back to bed.

In 1901, Robert Frost inherited the farm and a $500-a-year lifetime annuity from his grandfather. In 1902, he received the first payment of the annuity. Over the years, Frost kept up a dwindling poultry business. In 1906, he took a job teaching at Pinkerton Academy, a local private school, earning his first regular salary. By 1909, he sold off the last of the Wyandotte hens and the cow. He no longer cut hay or harvested the fruit trees.

Backed up by a regular salary and his inheritance, Frost borrowed money using the farm as collateral. The family finally had a little extra money and the energy to make some improvements. They had lived without new things for so long, that they were enthusiastic about their modest purchases, a new bookcase for the front parlor, an oak armchair with green-and-black-striped cushions for the sitting room, a multicolor sofa cover, and a new carpet.

In 1907, they took their first vacation in four years. The summer in the White Mountains relieved Frost's severe hay fever and gave them all a change. In 1909, Frost persuaded Elinor to rent the farm and move to Derry village.

Beginning in 1912, his annuity from his grandfather increased from $500 to $800 a year; he was earning $1000 at Pinkerton Academy and was getting some recognition for his poetry and teaching.

Frost was ready to sell the farm, but he couldn't find a buyer. The house was in bad repair. Frost had never painted it, and its roof needed reshingling. He had taken out two mortgages on the farm, and still owed interest on the first. In 1911, when he paid the $568.75 interest on the first mortgage, taken out in 1906, he was finally able to get rid of the farm by finding a real estate broker who would take over the second mortgage.

Elinor hated leaving. After giving up part of herself to her family, she had found fulfillment in having them with her in the close and intense isolation of the farm. Years later, in 1938, just before her death, she asked her husband to scatter her ashes in Hyla Brook.

Twenty-nine years after they had left Derry, Frost returned to do her bidding. But, by 1938, new owners had turned the farm into an auto-salvage business. When Frost returned, he found wrecked automobiles and unfriendly owners, who grudgingly allowed him to walk along Hyla Brook. There were traces of the past: a plank seat he had made for Elinor between two pine trees, a dam he had built with the children, now broken. But, the farm was so changed he could not leave her ashes.

In 1965, the United States Division of Parks and Recreation bought the farm, and between 1965 and 1975, added an additional seventy acres as a protective barrier. The restored farmhouse was opened to the public in 1976.

Frost Place

Franconia, New Hampshire

Robert Frost

Robert Frost

Ridge Road
Franconia, New Hampshire 03580
603-823-8038
603-823-5510 (poet-in-residence)

Open Memorial Day-June 30, 1-5 pm, weekends; July and August, 1-5 pm,
Tuesday through Sunday; Labor Day-October 12, 1-5 pm, Weekends.
Admission—Senior Citizens, $1.25; Adults, $1.75; Children 6-15, $1.00;
Children under 6, no charge. First editions of Frost's books, photographs,
memorabilia, and a collection of Frost's Christmas-card poems. Slide show:
"Robert Frost of Franconia." Self-guided natural history and poetry trail.
Poet in residence each summer, poetry readings held in the barn. Call
ahead for information about special events and exhibits.

1874. Born in San Francisco, California on March 26 to Isabella Moody
Frost and William Prescott Frost, Jr.
1885. RF's father dies, moves with his mother and sister to New
Hampshire.
1895. RF marries Elinor Miriam White, a former classmate at Lawrence
High School in Lawrence, Massachusetts.
1896. RF's son, Elliott, born.
1899. Daughter Lesley is born. RF withdraws from Harvard after two
years.
1900. First child, Elliott, dies of cholera. Frosts move to Derry, New
Hampshire in October.
1906. RF begins teaching at Pinkerton Academy in Derry.
1909. Frost family leaves Derry farm and moves to Derry Village.
1913. RF goes to England with family. His first two books are published
in England.
1915. RF moves to farm in Franconia, New Hampshire.
**1920. RF moves from Franconia to South Shaftsbury,
Vermont.**
1923. RF wins Pulitzer Prize for *New Hampshire*.
1930. Daughter Marjorie dies of puerperal fever.
1938. Elinor Frost dies.
1940. Carol, his only surviving son, commits suicide.
1942. RF wins his fourth Pulitzer Prize for *The Witness Tree*.
1961. RF reads "The Gift Outright" at John F. Kennedy's inauguration.
1963. Dies in Boston on January 29.

In February 1915, Robert Frost returned with his family from a three-year stay in England, where he had succeeded in getting his first two books of poetry published and enthusiastically reviewed. Just a few days before his ship docked in New York, *North of Boston* was finally published in America. Frost didn't know if Americans would love, hate, or be totally indifferent to the book.

Frost was unsettled. He had no place to live. Except for an $800-a-year annuity, he had no regular income. He and Elinor decided to look for a house north of Boston in Franconia, New Hampshire, a small village high in the White Mountains. They wanted to recapture the privacy they had known in the early years of their marriage. Between 1906 and 1910 they has spent four summers vacationing at the Lynch Family farm, where they returned and rented rooms, while they looked for a home of their own.

In April of 1915, the Frosts found a fifty-acre upland farm on Ore Hill, with a view of Mt. Lafayette. Robert Frost walked into the yard and introduced himself to the owner, Willis Herbert. As luck would have it, Herbert just happened to want a larger farm and was happy to sell the farm to the Frosts for $1,000. Later, when Herbert saw Frost's picture in a Boston newspaper and realized that he was no ordinary farmer, he demanded more money, but Frost kept him to the original price.

The Frosts moved to the farm in June 1915. There was no indoor bathroom and no furnace. Water was supplied by a mountain spring. But, there were plenty of advantages: clear pollen-free air, good for Frost's hay fever, and a dramatic view. Behind the barn, there were uphill pastures, a hayfield, wood-lots of tamarack, poplar, birch and sugar maple, and a sugar house.

Although the newspapers called him a farmer-poet, Frost was not a farmer and did only what farm work suited him or what he couldn't avoid. Frost finally succeeded in milking the balky cow by tying her at head and feet. In exchange for a share of the syrup, Frost got Willis Herbert to tap the sugar maples and do the sugaring, so that Frost was free to do as much or as little of the work as he liked. Sometimes, Frost would sit up all night in the sugar house keeping the wood fire going under the pan of boiling sap, but mostly, he avoided farmwork. He put in a vegetable garden but lost most of the harvest, since he hadn't protected the vegetables from early frost. The villagers saw him as a poet and a teacher and elected him president of the local Parent-Teachers' Association.

He and Elinor liked to let things go. He slept late, and she cleaned house only when she had to. They wanted to live on the land without working too hard. At first, Frost thought he would be able to earn enough from royalties, readings, and talks.

North of Boston, a best-seller in its fourth printing by the summer of 1915, made Frost a well-known and widely-written-about poet. Critics and reporters treated him as the successor to Whitman.

Frost was forty-one. Having lived in obscurity for so long, and having for years unsuccessfully tried to publish in magazines, he was now treated as an important person, and Elinor, as his wife, was entertained by people she would never have met if her husband hadn't published *North of Boston*. After hard times in Derry and in England, the Frosts enjoyed the deference and diversion. But Frost became crazed with success, and Elinor told him that he should quit running around to literary parties, scheming to be number one poet in America, and get back to his writing. She also wanted him to herself. She felt that his poems were a private matter between the two of them, and she didn't want to share her husband or his poems with the public.

They fought. She accused him of pandering to his public by refusing to be open about his religious doubts because he was afraid of losing readers. He gained from Elinor's antagonism, writing many poems in anger, despair, or reconciliation after one of their violent encounters.

Elinor's repeated pregnancies added to the tensions of their marriage. In the fall of 1915, in Franconia, she was pregnant again. Frost was happily relieved when she miscarried; he took care of the house and children while Elinor recovered. They did not want any more children, but they couldn't bring themselves to discuss birth control. Of her previous six pregnancies, four children had survived. During her first pregnancy, in 1896, her doctor had warned her that she had a weak heart and should avoid having children. What they may have gained in occasional instinctual lovemaking without birth control, they lost later in bitterness and resentment. In 1938, sick with heart disease and on her deathbed, Elinor blamed Frost for the repeated pregnancies which had destroyed her health and refused to see him.

They also fought about the children. Lesley, 16, Carol, 13, and Marjorie, 10, were all interested in writing. Elinor was angry with her husband for deliberately and jealously discouraging them. The children were perhaps less conscious of this discouragement. Lesley could stand up to her father, but Carol, who later committed suicide, became depressed from his father's constant nagging and fault-finding.

Luckily, the children enjoyed outdoor life. They gathered and transplanted wildflowers as they had in Derry, and picked highbush and lowbush blueberries, which were plentiful in Franconia.

Such country pastimes and the quiet of the farm were the reasons Frost had chosen Franconia. But he couldn't settle down to his writing. Recognition had activated his deeply competitive nature. He wanted to be the greatest poet in America; he couldn't bear the critics ranking Edward Arlington Robinson above him. To Frost's credit, he admitted his jealousy, even as he urged his reviewer friends to do his dirty work and criticize poets he hated.

In 1916, he wrote to Louis Untermeyer, a friend and fellow poet, that he felt like a "salesman" and that, "The poet in me died nearly ten years ago." Frost was afraid he had run out of inspiration. He had promised his publisher a new book, but the poems came slowly. Fame made him self-conscious. He worried about writing poems equal to his best.

Yet despite these fears, he managed to put a new book together. Of the thirty-two poems of *Mountain Interval*, thirteen were written in Bethlehem and Franconia, between 1915 and 1916, including his famous poem, "The Road Not Taken." Lesley typed the manuscript for her father. He wrote in longhand in the untidy first-floor study which faced Mt. Lafayette. In mountain temperatures that dropped to twenty-five degrees below zero, Frost kept warm with a huge almost ceiling-high cylindrical woodstove. He used his desk as a drop for papers and books and preferred writing in a Morris chair with a slanted board resting on the chair's arms. He had no set times for writing—when poems came, they came.

The royalties from his poetry and the fees from his readings were not a secure income. In January 1917, Frost began teaching at Amherst College at a salary of $2000 a year. For the next two years, the Frosts wintered in Amherst and summered in Franconia. Although the teaching job solved Frost's money problems, and Amherst treated him very well, awarding him an honorary degree and requiring him to teach only one semester beginning in the fall of 1918, he felt out of place in the liberal environment and far away from poetry. He wanted a poet's life, outside of institutions.

He resigned from Amherst in January 1920 and came back to Franconia with a new plan. His son, Carol, wanted to be a farmer. If the Frosts bought another farm where the winters were less harsh and Carol could raise a cash crop of apples, Frost could go on with his writing and poetry readings, without worrying about money. The Frosts planned to stay on in Franconia until they found another farm.

In 1915, while he was waiting to find the right property, he met Raymond Holden, a young, aspiring poet. Holden, who was wealthy, decided he wanted to live like his mentor. In 1919, he bought the upper twenty-five acres of the Frost farm for $2,500 and began building a house. He agreed to Frost's terms: if ever Frost wanted to sell the other half of the farm, Holden would buy it for another $2,500. When Holden made this agreement, he was looking foward to living next to the poet he admired and had no idea that Frost was already planning to leave Franconia. Frost shrewdly sized up this wealthy young man and took advantage of him. In the summer of 1920, as the Holdens moved into their new house, the Frosts were moving out.

The family was on the road again, on their way to South Shaftsbury, Vermont, with a new farm in mind and a new plan. Frost returned to Franconia for the summer of 1921 and lived in the old farmhouse which Holden generously lent him. Although the Frosts had bought a farm in Vermont, they abandoned the idea of farming, and in the fall of 1921, left for the University of Michigan where Frost had been made a Fellow of Letters.

In 1976, the town of Franconia bought Frost Place, which they maintain as a visitors' center and a summer residence for guest poets.

Maine

The
Sarah Orne Jewett
House

South Berwick, Maine

Sarah Orne Jewett

Sarah Orne Jewett

Route 236
South Berwick, Maine 03908
207-384-5269

Open June 1-October 15; 12 noon-5 pm; Tuesday, Thursday, Saturday, Sunday. Admission—Adults, $2.00; Children 6-12, $1.00; Children under 6, no charge. On-street parking. Outstanding example of Georgian architecture. Photographs, memorabilia of the Jewett family, and Sarah Orne Jewett, whose room is remarkably preserved.

1849. Born September 3, South Berwick, Maine to Caroline Perry Jewett and Theodore Jewett.
1865. SOJ graduates from Berwick Academy.
1869. SOJ's first story published in the *Atlantic Monthly*.
1877. SOJ's first book, *Deephaven* is published.
1878. SOJ's father dies.
1880. SOJ meets Annie Adams Fields with whom she formed a "Boston marriage."
1881. SOJ's first trip to Europe.
1892. SOJ's mother dies.
1896. *The Country of the Pointed Firs* published.
1897. SOJ's sister, Caroline Jewett Eastman, dies.
1901. SOJ is first woman to be awarded Doctor of Letters by Bowdoin College.
1902. SOJ is thrown from her carriage and suffers serious spinal concussion.
1909. Dies on June 26, in South Berwick, Maine.

Captain Theodore Jewett lived high on the fortune he had made in the West Indian trade. In 1839, he bought a house in South Berwick, Maine. The Georgian mansion, built in 1774, dominated the town square and was one of the most important houses in the town. The interior detail satisfied the captain's lavish taste for beauty, not utility. The paneled wainscotting, dentellated cornices, fluted columns, carved balusters, and newel posts were most elaborate in the front hall and stairs, the carving of which took three men 100 days to complete. The captain's son, Theodore, and Theodore's wife moved into the house just before their daughter, Sarah Orne Jewett, was born.

Jewett spent her first six years in a treasure house. Her grandfather, the captain, would come back from his voyages with furniture and china, among them Chippendale tables, chairs made for Charles I, Chinese vases, and Lowescroft china. The bold, florid, velvet, maroon-and-pink flock wallpaper, dotted with glitter, in the master bedroom had been seized by an American privateer in the War of 1812, before it could reach the governor of the West Indies.

In 1855, Sarah Orne Jewett moved to the house next door with her family. The two houses, separated by a lawn and enclosed by the same wooden slat fence, made a secure family compound, staffed by a platoon of servants. In back, there were barns, sheds, a vegetable garden, and open country fields filled with wildflowers.

She visited the old house often, spending much of her time with her grandmother. At twenty, inspired by a story her grandmother told her, she went back home to her desk, wrote all night, and sent the story off to the *Atlantic Monthly*, where it was later published.

Jewett, her parents, and two sisters moved back into the old house after the death of her uncle, William, in 1877. Soon after they moved in, they expanded the attic by adding three dormers. They contructed a long, trellised, brick walk from the back door to the garden. Jewett and her older sister, Mary, developed the garden, the only area which could stand more elaboration. They covered the trellis with densely twining honeysuckle and planted more of everything within box borders: lilies, larkspur, asters, peonies, poppies, roses, holly-hocks, French pinks, Mignonette, tulips, and daffodils.

Sarah Orne Jewett chose the plain, masculine back bed-room with its green-stained woodwork. She arranged all her childhood mementoes, which included her baby chair, stuffed animals, and an old, black school slate carved with her initials. Above the fireplace, she hung her riding whips, skates, and the small lantern she used when skating at night.

Jewett's social life was not much different from that of any other upper-middle-class young woman in South Berwick. She went to church on Sundays, wrote letters almost every day, paid formal calls each afternoon, eating cake with her white gloves on, and, sometimes, in the evenings, saw her friends at church socials or meetings of the girls' club where all the well-dressed ladies played euchre and acted charades.

In her early twenties, however, she realized she was differ-ent from most women. Her friends were marrying, but she wasn't interested in men, and her attraction to women made her feel odd, separate, and bad. At this time, she found comfort in religion and was baptized into the Episcopal Church. She also found a group of friends in Boston and Newport who were like her, single women with money, whom Jewett described as "willful-looking-brave-looking little fellows."

She wasn't interested in housekeeping. Her sister, Mary, managed the house as her mother got older, dealt with trades-people, directed the servants in their daily jobs and in the ferocious ritual of spring cleaning. It was Mary who put away the heavy sleigh robes when the snow melted, oversaw the laying of a new stable floor, and made sure every pair of curtains stayed white.

Jewett and her sister shared the garden work and would often eat their breakfast together under the arbor of honey-suckle with all the flowers around them.

In 1878, Jewett's father died. At first, she felt a wild rush of grief, then a depression she could not see the end of. For all her independence, Jewett, above all things, had been her father's daughter. She had been a sickly child, and her father, who was a doctor, had bundled her into his carriage and taken her on his country rounds for fresh air, discussing his cases and sharing his life with her. At one time, she wanted to be a doctor. Later, when she showed an interest in writing, he guided her. She thought of writing as their joint enterprise. After he had died, she wrote that she had lost the opportunity to express his "great thoughts."

Annie Fields filled the gap in her life. They became friends in 1880 when Jewett visited Annie and her husband, James Fields, in their summer home in Manchester, Massachusetts. During that visit, Jewett and Annie traveled to the Isles of Shoals. Annie was 46 and Jewett, 31. When James died in 1881, Jewett spent all winter with Annie in her home in Boston at 148 Charles Street. That spring, the two women took the first of many trips to Europe together.

In Annie, Jewett found a beautiful mother-muse who legitimized her sexual feelings by connecting them to her spiritual affinity to older people, the inspiration of much of her writing. Jewett felt Annie brought out her strongest side. She also needed to be mothered. She never gave up her childhood nicknames, and in her letters to Annie, deliberately kept the language of childhood: Sarah was "Pinny" and Annie was "Fuff." At forty-eight, she wrote from the house in South Berwick, "This is my birthday and I am always nine years old." With Annie, Jewett was both the child and the active lover. She wrote to Annie that she wanted "to paint things, and drive things, and *kiss* things."

Jewett got what she wanted. Winter and summer, she lived with Annie in Boston and Manchester-by-the-Sea, or they traveled abroad. In the spring, when the mud had dried and the roads were good for horseback riding, Jewett returned to South Berwick. There were fewer distractions there, and she had more time to write. There were still formal calls to be made in the afternoon, but after supper, Jewett went to bed early.

She was fresh in the morning for her writing. She thought of herself as an artist perfecting her craft. No longer afraid of being called selfish, she isolated herself every day at the Sheraton secretary near the front window of the wide upstairs hall, reworking the rough drafts of the stories she had written in bed when the ideas first occurred to her. At eye-level, she pinned up a motto from Flaubert, "*Ecrire la vie ordinaire comme on ecrit l'histoire."* ("Write about ordinary life as if you were writing history.")

Her books sold well, and success, which came easily with her first book, *Deephaven*, in 1877, continued to her twentieth and last book in 1905.

Sarah Orne Jewett remained active and physical. With the royalties from her first book, she bought a fast thoroughbred mare, which she named Sheila. Though she had become heavy, she still skated and, at the age of fifty, once borrowed a sled from some children and, she wrote, slid "over that pound-cake frosting of a coast most splendid."

After writing all day until dark, she would walk up Powder-house Hill and watch the moon rise. In the afternoons, she sometimes took Sheila out over old roads.

Annie would come up in the spring. She and Jewett had a talent for appreciating good moments and not brooding over the bad ones. The entertainment could be as simple as a picnic with bread and butter and watercress they pulled from a stream.

In South Berwick, Jewett was surrounded by caretakers, but she had responsibilities. By careful management of her royalties, she, unlike her sisters, Mary and Caroline, had increased the family fortune by $75,000.

Caroline Eastman Jewett moved in with Sarah and Mary after the death of her husband. When Caroline died in 1897, Jewett and Mary had their nephew Ned Eastman to look after. The two aunts brought him up, educated him, and made sure that, like all the Jewetts, he knew how to ride a fine horse.

In 1902, in South Berwick, Jewett was thrown from the carriage she was driving and never fully recovered from a spinal concussion. She died at home after a stroke on June 25, 1909.

Mary Jewett continued to live in the old house until her death in 1930. Her heir, Ned Eastman, died only a few months after his aunt and left the house to the Society for the Preservation of New England Antiquities.

The Wadsworth-Longfellow House

Portland, Maine

Henry Wadsworth Longfellow

Henry Wadsworth Longfellow

487 Congress Street
Portland, Maine 04101
207-772-1807
207-774-1822

Open June-September, 10 am-4 pm, Tuesday through Saturday.
Admission—Adults, $2.00; Children under 12, $1.00. Parking in nearby
municipal lot off Congress Street. Restrooms next door at Maine Historical Society building. Mementoes, furniture, portraits. Carefully preserved,
especially the eighteenth-century kitchen. Perennial garden restored and
maintained by Longfellow Garden Club.

**1807. Born February 7, in Portland, Maine to Zilpah Wads-
worth and Stephen Longfellow.**
1825. HWL graduates from Bowdoin College.
1826. HWL travels to Europe for a three-year study trip.
1829. Bowdoin names HWL Professor of Modern Languages.
1831. On September 14, HWL marries Mary Storer Potter of Portland,
Maine.
1836. Mary Potter Longfellow dies in Europe where HWL had gone to
study. HWL becomes Professor of Modern Languages at Harvard.
1839. *Voices of the Night* and *Hyperion*, HWL's first two books, are
published.
1843. On July 13, HWL marries Frances Appleton.
1844. Charles, the first of six children, is born, June 9.
1847. *Evangeline* published.
1854. HWL resigns from Harvard.
1855. *The Song of Hiawatha* is published.
1861. Fanny Appleton Longfellow dies in fire.
1882. Dies March 24.

Fresh from his service as a general in the Revolutionary War, Peleg Wadsworth, Henry Wadsworth Longfellow's grandfather, bought one-and-a-half acres, on what was then the grassy outskirts of Portland, for one hundred pounds, and built a barn and general store. In 1785, he began building a house on the same property. It was the first brick house in Portland, and the workmen, inexperienced in building brick houses, underestimated the number of bricks needed. The late-colonial-style house, finished in 1786 with a second shipment of bricks from Philadelphia, was built like a fortress. Its walls were sixteen inches thick, more than twice the thickness of ordinary construction.

In decorating the interior, Peleg Wadsworth put his money into the carved woodwork of the dining room and the parlor, where he was likely to entertain. In contrast, the two rooms at the back of the house, the kitchen and General Wadsworth's office, were small and plain. The rustic office had the widest floor boards in the house and dark, simulated-hardwood-grain woodwork. There was no mantel above the fireplace, just a squared-off molding. The Wadsworths took the bedroom over the parlor, reserving the large room over the dining room for guests. General Wadsworth's six children squeezed into the two upstairs back bedrooms. The general's wife, Elizabeth Bartlett Wadsworth, gave birth to four more children in the Portland house.

In 1804, the Wadsworth's eldest daughter, Zilpah, married Stephen Longfellow in the Fancy Parlor at the Portland House. Stephen Longfellow, the son of a judge, was a lawyer and later became a selectman, member of Congress, and a trustee of Bowdoin College. Both the Wadsworths and Longfellows were wealthy and socially prominent. Their Puritan ancestors had come over on the Mayflower.

Stephen and Zilpah Longfellow lived with the Wadsworths for a year before setting up on their own. Then, in 1807, they moved back with their sons, Stephen and Henry. That same year, General Wadsworth moved to an eight-thousand acre estate in Hiram, Maine, given to him by the government for his war service. He kept the deed to the Portland House during his lifetime, but, upon his death, left the house to his two daughters, Lucia and Zilpah. Lucia, who always had lived in the Portland house, continued to live there with her sister and brother-in-law.

Stephen Longfellow turned the dining room into a law office and added an entrance, so clients and law students could come and go without disturbing the house. The family used the General's old office for a dining room.

Henry Wadsworth Longfellow was eight months old when his family moved into his grandfather's house. From the time he was an infant, his mother noticed that he enjoyed music, and loved to be danced around the room and held up to see the bright polished balls which decorated one of the mirrors. Henry was influenced more by his mother's love for poetry than his grandfather's uniforms, pistols, and pistol cases. He disliked hunting and sports. Zilpah and her sister, Lucia, encouraged Henry's musical talent and his early efforts at writing.

The spirit of the house was artistic. No longer bound by strict Puritanism, Zilpah knew that music and dancing would not corrupt her children. A music teacher came to the house to give the children lessons on the Wadsworth spinet harpsichord, the first in Portland. The children took dancing lessons as well, sometimes twice a week, and showed off their skill at exhibition balls.

The Longfellows were a loving and disciplined family. Zilpah told Henry that his seven brothers and sisters were dear friends sent to him by God. Each evening, the family gathered in the small back dining room which had been General Wadsworth's office. Lucia and Zilpah read, knit, or sewed, while the older children sat around the table in front of the fire and studied and the young ones played noisily under the table. Longfellow never saw his mother idle. She could knit and read at the same time, but sewing took all her attention. By the time Zilpah was eight she had learned to use a needle with enough skill to finish a sampler demonstrating all the stitches in her repertory, and later passed on her craft to her four daughters. Her eight-year-old daughter Mary's sampler reads, "Count that day lost whose low descending sun/Views from thy hand no virtuous action done." Work and virtue went along with music and dancing.

The Longfellows encouraged grace, but not softness. Zilpah expected her children to sit at a table when they read or studied. If they stretched out on the floor in front of the fire, she thought them indolent. They read novels with their parents' consent, but the girls decided that the new ladies' magazines were trashy.

Novel-reading was forbidden on Sundays. The Longfellows still kept the Sabbath in the old way. All weekday occupations stopped. They went to the Congregational Meeting House twice a day but not on Christmas, which was celebrated only by Catholics and Episcopalians. In winter, Longfellow carried the footstove to church and, in spring and summer, bunches of flowers, apple-blossoms, or pinks. In the afternoon, Zilpah read from the family Bible; the children learned family history by reading and asking questions about the long list of family births and deaths. They saw their names in fresh ink, the names of their ancestors beginning to fade. In the evening, they sang hymns.

Despite discomfort, the family held on to old ways with a traditional austerity that seemed almost patrician. While Longfellow lived there, there was never any indoor plumbing in the house. During his childhood, Zilpah or Lucia bathed him in a shallow tin tub front of the kitchen fire, above which his night clothes warmed in a cupboard against the chimney. He slept under a feather quilt in an unheated bedroom on the third floor, which his father had added to the house in 1815. It was so cold at the top of the house, water froze in the pitcher on his washstand.

There were no fires in the office at night and none in the parlor, except when company came. Even so, they burned up to thirty cords of wood a year in the open fireplaces, which they used for heating and cooking. They tried to make the house tighter by jamming wedges between the windows and frames.

In 1821, at the age of fourteen, Longfellow left home to go to Bowdoin College, thirty-five miles from Portland. He was terribly homesick, and his family missed him. His mother wrote often. His father sent cases of apples and nuts, and his sister Anne, still at home, sent boxes of gingerbread.

Sometimes, he couldn't get home for winter vacations because of bad weather, but he was sure to be home on July 4, which Portland celebrated with parties, speeches, poems, a special oration, and the reading of the Declaration of Independence.

In the fall of 1825, he graduated from Bowdoin, fourth in his class. He wanted to be a writer, but his father expected him to choose law, medicine, or the ministry.

Shortly after commencement, Bowdoin offered Longfellow a professorship in Modern Languages, with the provision that he study in Europe. His father was satisfied that he would earn a secure living and agreed to finance the trip. Longfellow, hoping to combine scholarship with writing, was relieved to avoid a family breach. He wanted his father on his side, and between the fall of 1825 and the spring of 1826, when he left for Europe, he even read law in his father's office in Portland.

But his real love was poetry. With Zilpah's and Lucia's encouragement, he had been writing poems since he was a boy, publishing an early effort in the *Portland Gazette* when he was thirteen. He continued writing at Bowdoin, and he found a reception in *The United States Literary Gazette*, which, in 1825, published seventeen of his poems. At home for almost a year before leaving for Europe, he worked in the Little Room, a tiny, closet-like space next to his father's office, where he pushed aside the law books for poetry. Stephen Longfellow, who read these early poems, advised his son to take greater pains and revise more carefully.

In letters, his father reminded him about the necessity for work, and Zilpah warned him against vice. After three years in Europe, Longfellow returned fluent in French, Italian, and Spanish and became professor of Modern Languages at Bowdoin.

Throughout his life, Longfellow returned to the family home in Portland. These visits touched off poems about his lost youth. He wrote in the third-floor guest room at the top of the house, or in the back room on the first floor, where, as a child, he had sat with his family while he did his lessons. The city was crowding up around the house, but inside, little had changed—no toilets and no bathtubs with running water. They used well water until 1865, when they installed a kitchen pump. Portland outlawed outhouses within the city boundaries, but Longfellow's sister Anne Longfellow Pierce, who came back to live at the house after her husband died, had gotten a special permit to keep the Wadsworth-Longfellow outhouse.

Anne was a preserver and a saver—furniture, tiny infant shirts sewed by her mother, every one of the many children's christening caps, embroidered handkerchiefs from her trousseau, family papers and receipts.

She lived with her familiar and treasured possessions until her death in 1901, leaving the house and all its contents to the Maine Historical Society, which opened the house to the public in 1901.

Other Places of Literary Interest

Connecticut

Cheshire

Amos Bronson Alcott lived at 10 Main Street with uncle, who ran Cheshire Academy.

Cornwall

James Thurber lived at the large colonial house adjacent to the Mohawk State Forest, 1945-1961.

Greenwich

Clare Booth Luce and *Henry Luce* lived at 1275 King Street, which they bought in 1935.

Hadlyme

160 Ardmore Street, home of poet Donald Hall.

Thornton Wilder built home at 50 Deepwood Drive, 1929.

Hartford

Nook Farm, intersection of Forest Street and Farmington Avenue, tract of 140 acres with homes of people prominent in the Arts, *William Gillette, Harriet Beecher Stowe, Mark Twain, Charles Dudley Warner.*

25 Belknap Road, home of *Sinclair Lewis.*

Wallace Stevens worked at Hartford Accident and Indemnity Company, 690 Asylum Street; lived at 118 Westerly Terrace; buried at Cedar Hill Cemetery, 453 Fairfield Avenue.

Kent

James Gould Cozzens was graduated from Kent School in 1922.

Lakeville

Archibald MacLeish and *John Hersey* were students at Hotchkiss School.

Litchfield

Birthplace of *Harriet Beecher Stowe* marked by plaque.

New Haven

Louis Auchincloss, Joel Barlow, Stephen Vincent Benet, William Rose Benet, James Fenimore Cooper, Clarence Day, Jonathan Edwards, John Hersey, Sinclair Lewis, Archibald MacLeish, Royall Tyler, Robert Penn Warren, Noah Webster, and *Thornton Wilder* were students at Yale University.

Redding

The Mark Twain Library, Route 53, memorabilia, first editions, and photographs of *Samuel Clemens*.

Ridgefield

Flannery O'Connor lived with writers *Robert* and *Sally Fitzgerald* at 70 Acre Road, 1949-50.

Eugene O'Neill lived at Brook Farm, 845 North Salem Road, 1922-23.

Stamford

141 Downs Avenue, home of *Maxwell Anderson,* 1955-1959.

233 Stamford Avenue, home of *Mary McCarthy* and *Edmund Wilson,* late 1930s-early 1940s.

Wallingford

Edward Albee and *John Dos Passos* were students at Choate School.

Eugene O'Neill recovered from tuberculosis at Gaylord Hospital.

Waterbury

Hayden Carruth was born at 58 Central Avenue, August 3, 1921.

Waterford

The Eugene O'Neill Theater Center, Route 213, summer theater conferences, letters and furniture of *Eugene O'Neill.*

West Hartford

Wallace Stevens lived at 735 Farmington Avenue with his wife and daughter, 1924-32.

227 South Main Street (P), birthplace of *Noah Webster,* now a museum open to the public.

Westport

244 South Compo Drive, home of *F. Scott Fitzgerald* and Zelda Fitzgerald, 1920.

82 King's Highway, home of *Jerome Weidman,* 1948-61.

Wolcott

Beach Road and Spindle Hill Road, birthplace of *Amos Bronson Alcott*, marked by plaque.

Woodbury

595 Main Street, childhood home of *Hayden Carruth*.

Rhode Island

Newport

Bret Harte lived at the Newbold Edgar Villa on Harrison Avenue, 1870s; the building is currently the Village House Convalescent Home.

As a young man, *Henry James* lived with his family at 463-465 Spring Street and at 13-15 Kay Street.

Edith Wharton lived at Land's End.

Providence

Nathanael West and *S. J. Perelman* were students at Brown University.

54 College Street, home of *James Fenimore Cooper*, now owned by Brown University.

The Providence Atheneum, 251 Benefit Street, collection of *Edgar Allan Poe* letters and photographs.

Woonsocket

247 Gaskill Street, home of *Edwin O'Connor*.

Massachusetts

Amherst

249 South Pleasant Street, childhood home of poet, novelist *Helen Hunt Jackson*.

Andover

80 Bartlett Street (moved from Chapel Avenue), home of *Harriet Beecher Stowe*, 1853-1864.

Belmont

90 Somerset Street, home of *William Dean Howells*, 1878-181, National Historic Landmark.

Beverly

Birthplace of poet *Lucy Larcom*, 1824-1893; room devoted to her life and writings at the Beverly Historical Society, 117 Cabot Street.

Boston

Louisa May Alcott, lived at 20 Pinckney Street in the 1850s; moved with her family to 10 Louisburg Square in 1885; died at 2 Dunreath Place, Roxbury, 1888.

8 Arlington Street, offices of *The Atlantic Monthly.*

670 Baker Street, West Roxbury (P), site of nineteenth-century Utopian commune *Brook Farm.*

361 Park Street, home of *Richard Henry Dana, Jr.,* 1874-1880.

125 Highland Street, home of *William Lloyd Garrison,* 1864-1879, National Historic Landmark.

Edward Everett Hale, lived at 39 Highland Street, in the late 1850s and at 12 Morley Street, now offices of Research Institute of Africa and African Diaspora Arts, Inc.

Nathaniel Hawthorne lived at 54 Pinckney Street and 8 Somerset Place while working at the Boston Custom House, 1839-1841; married at 13 West Street.

Oliver Wendell Holmes, Sr. lived at 164 Charles Street, 1859-1871 and 296 Beacon Street, 1871-1894.

13 Walnut Street, home of *Julia Ward Howe,* mid-1800s.

William Dean Howells lived at 4 Louisburg Square and 302 Beacon Street where he finished *The Rise of Silas Lapham* (1805).

Henry James lived at 13 Ashburton Place, 1865-1866.

Henry Wadsworth Longfellow married at 39 Beacon Street (P), July 13, 1843. Owned by Women's City Club.

97 Beacon Street, winter home of *Amy Lowell.*

91 Revere Street, childhood home of *Robert Lowell;* also lived at 170 and 239 Marlborough Street and at 33 Commonwealth Avenue.

43 West Cedar Street, home of *J. P. Marquand,* 1920s.

Cotton Mather, Increase Mather, and *Samuel Mather* buried in Copps Hill Burying Ground, Hull Street.

3 School Street, *The Old Corner Bookstore,* now The Globe Corner Book Store, owned by *James T. Fields* and *W.D. Ticknor,* founders of the publishing company Ticknor and Fields.

Eugene O'Neill died in the Shelton Hotel, November 27, 1953; building currently Shelton Hall, a Boston University dormitory.

60 School Street, *The Parker House,* meeting place of the Saturday Club, *William Ellery Channing, Richard Henry Daa, Jr., Ralph Waldo Emerson, Nathaniel Haw-thorne, Oliver Wendell Holmes, Henry James, Henry Wadsworth Longfellow, James Russell Lowell,* and *John Greenleaf Whittier.*

9 Willow Street, home of *Sylvia Plath,* 1950s.

55 Beacon Street, home of *William Prescott,* 1845-1859.

802 Beacon Street, family home of *George Santayana.*

Harriet Beecher Stowe lived with her family at 42 Green Street, 1826-1832.

Daniel Webster lived at 57 Mt. Vernon Street and 138 Summer Street.

Brookline

70 Heath Street, Sevenels, home of *Amy Lowell.*

Cambridge

Conrad Aiken lived at 8 Plympton Street, 1929. Houseguest *Malcolm Lowry* worked on *Ultra Marine* while visiting.

E.E. Cummings born at 104 Irving Street; lived at 6 Wyman Road.

Margaret Fuller born at 71 Cherry Street, May 23, 1812; lived at 42 Brattle Street in 1832.

37 Concord Avenue, home of *Oliver Wendell Holmes, Sr.*

20 Quincy Street, family home of *Henry James;* brother *William James* lived at 95 Irving Street.

33 Elmwood Avenue, life-long home of *James Russell Lowell.*

May Sarton lived at 10 Avon Street and 103 Ray-mond Street during her childhood; later, at 139 Oxford Street, 1945-1950, and 14 Wright Street, 1950-1957.

Richard Wilbur lived at 22 Plympton Street, 1945-1947 and at 37 Kirkland Street.

The Blacksmith House, 56 Brattle Street (P), home of the blacksmith who was the subject of *Longfellow's* "The Village Blacksmith." Mon-day evening poetry readings, except in summer.

Grolier Book Shop, 6 Plymp-ton Street (P), founded in 1927, visited by many famous writers, specializes in poetry.

James Agee, Conrad Aiken, Thomas Bailey Aldrich, Horatio Alger, Jr. Nathaniel Benchley, Robert Benchley, Van Wyck Brooks, James Gould Cozzens, Countee Cullen, John Dos Passos, W. E. B. DuBois, T. S. Eliot, Ralph Waldo Emerson, Robert Frost, Edward Hoagland, Norman Mailer, John P. Marquand, Cotton Mather, Increase Mather, Samuel Mather, Eugene O'Neill, John Reed, Adrienne Rich, George Ripley, Edwin Arlington Robinson, Louis Agassiz, William Ellery Channing, Mary Baker Eddy, Henry Wadsworth Longfellow, William Prescott, and William Dean Howells are all writers who have attended Harvard University.

Chicopee

91-93 Church Street, home of Edward Bellamy, from birth-1887. (P-by appointment).

Concord

The Concord Antiquarian Society Museum, 200 Lexington Road, furniture and memorabilia from Ralph Waldo Emerson's study and Henry David Thoreau's cabin at Walden.

The Concord Free Public Library, 129 Main Street, collection of Henry David Thoreau memorabilia, books, and surveying equipment.

49 Sudbury Road, home of Franklin Sanborn.

Henry David Thoreau born in house on Virginia Road, moved east of site and privately occupied, marked by plaque; lived at 255 Main, 1850-death, May 6, 1862; in 1877, house was bought by Louisa May Alcott for her sister Anna.

Thoreau Lyceum, 156 Belknap Street, Thoreau memorabilia and replica of cabin at Walden Pond.

Sleepy Hollow Cemetery, Route 62, burial place of Louisa May Alcott, William Ellery Channing, Ralph Waldo Emerson, Nathaniel Hawthorne, Henry David Thoreau, and Elizabeth Palmer Peabody

Haverhill

The Whittier Homestead, 305 Whittier Road (P), childhood home of John Greenleaf Whittier, setting of "Snowbound." Open to the public all year, Tuesday-Saturday, 9-5; Sunday, 1-5. Call for information: 617-373-3979.

Ipswich

Site of *Anne Broadstreet's* house at 33 High Street, marked by plaque.

John Updike lived at 26 East Street and 50 Labor-in-Vain Road.

Lenox

The Little Red House, reconstructed home of *Nathaniel Hawthorne*, Hawthorne Avenue (P), open to the public in summer, owner by Tanglewood-Berkshire Music Center.

Lowell

Jack Kerouac born March 12, 1922, 9 Lupine Street; lived at 33-35 Sarah Avenue, 1935-1938.

Medford

John Ciardi and *Archibald MacLeish* were students at Tufts University.

Nantucket

31 Pine Street, home of *Tennessee Williams* in the 1940s.

New Bedford

Herman Melville stayed with his sister at 100 Madison Street, now Swain School of Design, visited Seamen's Bethel, 15 Johnny Cake Hill. Sailed from New Bedford on whaler, *Acushnet*.

Newburyport

William Lloyd Garrison born at 5 School Street, December 10, 1805.

Northampton

23 Dryads Green, home of *George Washington Cable*, 1892-1925.

16 Paradise Road, home of *Mary Ellen Chase*.

Sylvia Plath attended Smith College, 1951-1955, lived in Haven House and Lawrence House.

Provincetown

571 Commercial Street, home of *John Dos Passos*. 1929-1947.

Harry Kemp lived at 577 Commercial Street and 15 Howland Street; replica of his shack on the dunes is at Provincetown Heritage Museum, 356 Commercial Street.

Norman Mailer lived at 565 Commercial Street, 1960s.

Henry David Thoreau lived at 9 Carver Street and, in 1855, at Gifford's Union House.

Quincy

John Cheever born at 43 Elm Street, May 27, 1912.

Rockport

Katherine Anne Porter completed *Ship of Fools* (1962) at the Yankee Clipper Inn, 127 Granite Street.

Salem

Anne Bradstreet lived at 126 Essex Street, 1630s, now site of the Essex Institute. *Nathaniel Hawthorne* born at 21 Union Street, July 4, 1804; house was moved to grounds of *The House of the Seven Gables*, 54 Turner Street (P), both are open to the public; Hawthorne also lived at 10 Herbert Street, 16 Chestnut Street, and 14 Mall, where he wrote *The Scarlet Letter*: these three houses are privately owned. *Salem Maritime National Historic Site*, 178 Derby Street (P), *Nathaniel Hawthorne*'s restored office where he worked in the Custom House, open to the public daily.

The Essex Institute, 126 Essex Street (P), collection of *Nathaniel Hawthorne* papers, open to the public.

Springfield

Dr. Seuss, Theodore Seuss Geisel, born 162 Summer Avenue, March 2, 1904.

Wayland

91 Old Sudbury Road, home of *Lydia Maria Child*; buried in North Cemetery.

Wellesley

23 Elmwood Road, home of *Sylvia Plath*, 1942.

Winthrop

92 Johnson Avenue, home of *Sylvia Plath*, 1930s and 1940s.

Williamstown

Thorvale Farm, Oblong Road, now home of the Novitiate of the Carmelite Fathers' Chapel, former home of *Sinclair Lewis*, 1946-1949.

Vermont

Arlington

Dorothy Canfield Fisher buried in St. James Cemetery, Main Street. The Martha Canfield Library, Main Street, collection of *Dorothy Canfield Fisher* memorabilia.

Barnard

Sinclair Lewis and *Dorothy Thompson* lived at Twin Farms.

Bennington

Faculty members of *Bennington College* included: *W.H. Auden, Bernard De Voto, Ralph Ellison, Stanley Kunitz, Bernard Malamud, Howard Nemerov,* and *Theodore Roethke.*

Brattleboro

Rudyard Kipling and his wife lived in Bliss Cottage on Kipling Road; also, in Naulakha, which Kipling designed, off Kipling Road, three miles northeast of town.

Burlington

Ethan Allen lived on farm now called Ethan Allen Park, off North Avenue. He died there on February 12, 1789. Buried in Greenmount Cemetery, Colchester Avenue.

Danby

Town was home of *Pearl Buck* in the 1970s.

East Poultney

Building where *Horace Greeley* worked as a printer's apprentice (P), 1826-1830, now *Horace Greeley Museum.* Open to the public in July and August.

Ferrisburg

Rokeby, Route 7 (P), home of *Rowland Evans Robinson* writer of nineteenth-century stories of Vermont life, now a museum open to the public.

Middlebury

Middlebury College Library, Robert Frost Room, books and papers relating to *Robert Frost.*

Old Bennington

Robert Frost buried in the cemetery located next to the Old First Church on Route 9.

Ripton

Route 125, farm owned by *Robert Frost,* 1940-1963, now owned by Middlebury College.

Robert Frost Wayside Recreation Area, Memorial Nature Trail just off Route 125.

South Shaftsbury

Robert Frost lived in The Stone House, 1919-1930, when he moved to The Gully.

Windsor

Editor *Maxwell Perkins* spent childhood summers at 26 North Main Street.

New Hampshire

Center Harbor

John Greenleaf Whittier vacationed at The Sturtevant House.

Concord

24 Spring Street, home of Ellen Louisa Tucker, first wife of *Ralph Waldo Emerson*, moved from its original location on Pleasant Street, where they were married.

Exeter

Graduates of Phillips Exeter Academy: *Robert Anderson, Robert Benchley, Booth Tarkington, and Gore Vidal*.

Hampton Falls

Grove House, formerly Elmfield, winter residence of *John Greenleaf Whittier*.

Hanover

Graduates of Dartmouth College: *Richard Eberhart, Budd Schulberg, George Ticknor,* and *Daniel Webster*.

Isles of Shoals

Site of Appledore Hotel, Appledore Island, owned by father of *Celia Thaxter*. Literary visitors included: *John Greenleaf Whittier, William Morris Hunt, Sarah Orne Jewett* and *Annie Adams Fields*. Ferry to islands available from Portsmouth.

Jaffrey

Henry David Thoreau camped on Mount Monadnock.

Jaffrey Center

Willa Cather buried in the Old Burying Yard.

North Hampton

Ogden Nash buried in Little River Cemetery on Atlantic Avenue.

Peterborough

Stephen Vincent Benet, Willa Cather, Edwin Arlington Robinson, as well as *Thornton Wilder, James Baldwin, Louise Bogan* and others were guests at the *MacDowell Colony*, a country retreat for artists.

Plymouth

Robert Frost lived in a cottage at corner of Highland Avenue and School Street, 1911-1912, while teaching at Plymouth Normal School.

Portsmouth

Thomas Bailey Aldrich born at 45 Court Street, November 11, 1836.
James T. Fields born at 83-85 Gate Street, Dec. 31, 1817.
Celia Thaxter born at 48 Daniel Street, June 29, 1835.

Walpole

Louisa May Alcott, lived in house formerly on Main Street, now at 83 High Street, 1855-1856.

Maine

Alna

Birthplace of *Edwin Arlington Robinson* (P). House open July and August, 2-4 pm, Wednesdays and Saturdays. Call ahead. (207) 586-5479.

Brunswick

44 Harpswell Street, home of *Robert Tristram Coffin. Nathaniel Hawthorne* lived at 25 Federal Street while at Bowdoin College.
76 Federal Street, home of *Henry Wadsworth Longfellow* and Mary Potter Longfellow, 1831-1835.
Harriet Beecher Stowe lived at 63 Federal Street, while her husband taught at Bowdoin.

Camden

Edna St. Vincent Millay lived with her mother at 82 Washington Street; The Whitehall Inn has an Edna St. Vincent Millay Reading Room.

Castine

House on corner of Perkins Street and Madockawando Street home of *Ellen Glasgow*.

Gardiner

67 Lincoln Avenue, child-
hood home of *Edwin Arlington Robinson,* from
birth-1891.

Hiram

Wadsworth Hall, home of
General Peleg Wadsworth,
grandfather of *Henry
Wadsworth Longfellow.*

Kennebunkport

Kenneth Roberts born in
the Storer Mansion on
Storer Street, December 8,
1885.
Booth Tarkington's summer
home Seawood on South
Main Street.

Rockland

Birthplace of *Edna St. Vincent Millay* marked by
plaque at 198-200 Broadway.